Warne Gerrard Guides for Walkers

HAMPSHIRE

AND THE NEW FOREST

WALKS FOR MOTORISTS

Roberta MacLaren

30 circular walks with sketch maps

FREDERICK WARNE

Published by
Frederick Warne (Publishers) Ltd
40 Bedford Square
London WC1B 3HE

© Frederick Warne (Publishers) Ltd 1982

The photograph on the front cover shows the New Forest near Rhinefield. The picture on the back cover is of the monument at Farley Mount.

Publishers' Note

While every care has been taken in the compilation of this book, the publishers cannot accept responsibility for any inaccuracies. Things may have changed since the book was published: paths are sometimes diverted, a concrete bridge may replace a wooden one, stiles disappear. Please let the publishers know if you discover anything like this on your way.

The length of each walk in this book is given in miles and kilometres, but within the text Imperial measurements are quoted. It is useful to bear the following approximations in mind: 5 miles = 8 kilometres, $\frac{1}{2}$ mile = 805 metres, 1 metre = 39.4 inches.

ISBN 0 7232 2169 3

Phototypeset by Butler & Tanner Ltd, Frome and London
Printed by Galava Printing Co., Ltd, Nelson, Lancashire

Contents

			Page
		Introduction	7
Walk	1	Waggoners Wells	12
	2	Eversley	15
	3	The Basingstoke Canal	18
	4	Odiham and Greywell	21
	5	Selborne	24
	6	Chawton Park Wood	28
	7	Hambledon – The Home of Cricket	31
	8	Silchester	35
	9	Cheriton	39
	10	Preston Candover	42
	11	Kingsclere and Watership Down	44
	12	Fawley Down	48
	13	Titchfield	50
	14	Shawford and St Catherine's Hill	54
	15	Calshot	58
	16	Longparish	61
	17	Farley Mount	64
	18	Denny Lodge	67
	19	Longstock	70
	20	Brockenhurst	73
	21	Rhinefield Ornamental Drive	77
	22	Keyhaven	80
	23	Holidays Hill Inclosure	82
	24	Rufus Stone	85
	25	Wilverley and the Naked Man	88
	26	Bolderwood	91
	27	Eyeworth Pond	95
	28	Woodgreen	98
	29	Breamore and the Mizmaze	101
	30	Martin Down	104

HAMPSHIRE

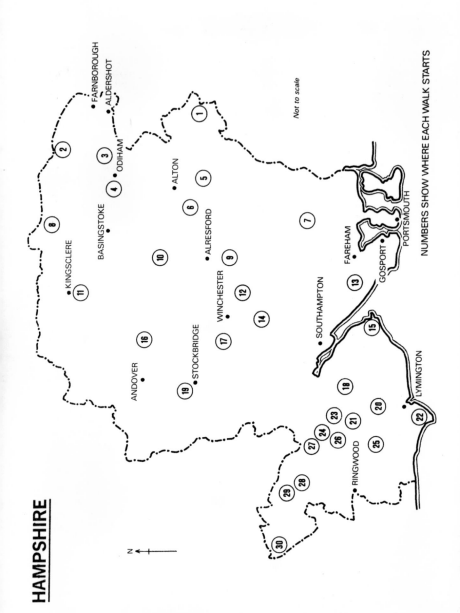

NUMBERS SHOW WHERE EACH WALK STARTS

Not to scale

Introduction

Situated in the centre of England's south coast, Hampshire is bordered by Dorset and Wiltshire in the west, Berkshire in the north and Surrey and West Sussex in the east. It is a county of sharp contrasts, its scenery including wide expanses of open heathland, dense woodland and softly rolling hills. It also has several large towns and rapidly developing industrial areas, such as Basingstoke and Andover, which are steadily encroaching into the surrounding farmland.

In the south the large commercial port of Southampton lies at the northern end of the Southampton Water at a point where the river Itchen flows into the sea. Southampton is the third most important port in England and handles more passenger traffic than any other port in the country. It also has one of the world's largest dry docks. A large oil refinery was built near Southampton in 1951 at Fawley on the western side of the Southampton Water (see Walk 13).

Southampton has been an important port since Roman times. Its fine natural harbour has the added advantage of a double tide which gives easy access to shipping. This is caused by the position of the Isle of Wight (see Walk 15) off the coast to the south of the Southampton Water.

Today Southampton is virtually joined by a great sprawl of houses to the towns of Gosport and Portsmouth further along the Hampshire coast to the east. These towns are two of the country's most important naval bases.

Yet, in spite of the swift growth of Hampshire's urban areas, much of the county is still unspoilt. Away from the towns and the fast main roads the peaceful villages and winding country lanes have a character and charm all of their own (see Walk 10).

In the east of the county, where the western extremity of the Weald stretches over the county border, the scenery is very reminiscent of that to be found in Surrey and West Sussex. Here there are high hills, many of which are called hangers, and areas of delightful woodland (see Walk 1).

This area of Hampshire abounds with a wide variety of wild life and it was here that Gilbert White, the famous naturalist, lived and studied (see Walk 5). Gilbert White was curate of Selborne during the eighteenth century and the village, together with its high hanger, still possesses many interesting reminders of this fascinating man.

In the north-west of the county are the Hampshire Downs, a range of high chalk hills stretching north into Berkshire. Their steep grassy slopes and open hilltops afford magnificent views across Hampshire and the neighbouring counties. Some of the downs are used for sheep farming or the growing of cereal crops but the training of racehorses is also a thriving industry here (see Walk 11).

Another belt of chalk downland runs across the middle of the county and here, once again, the views are delightful. To the east of Winchester is Fawley Down and Cheesefoot Head (see Walk 12). Cheesefoot Head is an impressive viewpoint rising to a height of 600 feet above sea level.

To the west of Winchester part of the downland is conserved as a country park (see Walk 17). The highest point in this area is Beacon Hill from which, on a clear day, it is possible to see the spire of Salisbury Cathedral in the west and the Isle of Wight in the south. Near the summit of Beacon Hill is one of the most curious monuments in the county. It is shaped like a small pyramid and was erected during the eighteenth century by a local landowner, Paulet St John, to the memory of his horse.

In the south-west of the county the scenery changes abruptly. Most of this area is covered by the New Forest, William of Normandy's finest legacy to the nation that he conquered and Hampshire's most popular tourist area. It was not long after the Norman Conquest that William decided to set aside this area of Hampshire as a royal hunting preserve. He often hunted in the forest and it was here that his successor, King William Rufus, so mysteriously met his death in 1100 (see Walk 24).

Because the forest was used for hunting, the local peasants were forbidden to erect fences and their domestic animals were allowed to roam freely in the forest. This practice gave rise to the commoners' rights that are in force today; cattle, pigs and donkeys still run free in the forest and mingle with the famous New Forest ponies.

These semi-wild ponies are also owned by the local residents and form an integral part of the area's economy. At Beaulieu Road station (see Walk 18) are the pens where they are auctioned at sales in April, August, September, October and November. At these times this usually quiet area of the forest comes alive with a bustle of activity as buyers, sellers and sight-seers gather together to watch the ponies being sold. New Forest ponies are greatly prized as children's riding ponies and, besides those sold to English families and stables, great numbers are sent to the continent for this purpose.

The number of animals running free in the forest also gave rise to another interesting old custom, that of pollarding trees. This was done by cutting the top section off the trunk thus ensuring that the branches grew low down so that the animals could eat the foliage. Although this custom is no longer practised there are still many examples of pollarded trees to be seen including the Knightwood Oak (see Walk 23), the oldest pollarded tree in the forest.

Some of the most beautiful of the forest scenery is to be found in the area around Eyeworth Pond (see Walk 27). Here conifers, planted by the Forestry Commission which controls large parts of the forest, stand side by side with the native oak woods and the open moorland affords panoramic views towards Salisbury in the north and Bournemouth in the west.

At Rhinefield (see Walk 21) the woodland has an added attraction for here there is an ornamental drive. This was laid out during the nineteenth century when the road it borders was merely a gravel drive that led to Rhinefield Lodge, the home of the Master Keeper. The ornamental drive consists of an avenue of magnificent conifers some of which are the tallest of their kind in the British Isles. The area around the Rhinefield Ornamental Drive has been laid out by the Forestry Commission as a series of forest walks and there are some more of these at Bolderwood (see Walk 26). Amongst the features included in this area is a deer sanctuary where special wooden hides enable visitors to watch the timid fallow deer.

Other types of deer are to be seen in the area around Brockenhurst (see Walk 20). This is another very lovely part of the forest and was the home of two of the New Forest's most famous characters, the eighteenth-century naturalist William Gilpin and Brusher Mills who made his living by catching snakes.

During Gilpin's life time the New Forest was a favourite haunt of smugglers who landed their cargoes on the Hampshire coast and brought them inland across the deserted wilderness of the forest. Near Wilverley Plain (see Walk 25) there is a track which the smugglers used and an old dead tree called the Naked Man which once served as a gallows.

Besides the wealth of delightful and very varied scenery Hampshire also possesses a long and interesting history. Because of its position on the south coast it was subject to invasions by nomadic tribes from the continent from the earliest prehistoric times. Many of these tribes made their way up the county's rivers such as the Avon (see Walk 28), and the Test (see Walk 16). Some left little trace of their passing whilst others built durable structures like Grim's Ditch (see Walk 30) and the hill-fort on Danebury Hill (see Walk 19).

Two of the most interesting early remains in the county are the fascinating mizmazes to be found on St Catherine's Hill (see Walk 14) and Breamore Down (see Walk 29). These mazes, consisting of intricate patterns of paths cut into the chalk, are amongst the few of their kind to be found in the British Isles. Nobody knows their exact age or their purpose but it is believed that they played an important part in religious rites practised here long before Christianity came to Britain.

The Romans also left their mark on Hampshire. Beneath the fields in the northern part of the county lie buried the remains of Calleva (see Walk 8), a town the Romans built on a site originally fortified by the Celts.

During the Saxon period Hampshire became part of the Kingdom of Wessex and for a time Winchester was the capital of England. This came to an end after the Norman Conquest when London was made the capital city but Winchester continued to hold a position of importance. Many of the English kings were frequent visitors here including John who built a castle at Odiham (see Walk 4) so that he could break his journeys between Winchester and Windsor. It was from this castle, one June day in 1215, that King John rode out to Runnymede to set his seal on the Magna Carta.

In 1501 another king came to Hampshire. He was Henry VII who accompanied his eldest son, Prince Arthur, to Dogmersfield (see Walk 3) to meet his future bride. She was Katherine of Aragon, who was destined to be widowed just five months after her wedding and then to marry Arthur's brother, King Henry VIII, and become the first of his six wives.

Hampshire was also the scene of many important events during the Civil War. At Cheriton (see Walk 9), a decisive battle was fought. It ended in a defeat from which the Royalist army never recovered and was the beginning of a chain of events leading to the downfall of King Charles I. When King Charles was a prisoner he was held for a while in Hurst Castle (see Walk 22). He was brought there from the Isle of Wight and was later removed to Windsor and then to London to stand trial.

During the latter half of the eighteenth century the Basingstoke Canal was built (see Walks 3 and 4). It was designed to carry goods from London to Basingstoke but was never a commercial success and soon fell into disuse. After years of neglect large parts of it are now being restored and there are many features of great interest to be seen, such as the Greywell Tunnel.

At about the time that the Basingstoke Canal was built another part of Hampshire was becoming famous for quite a different reason. This was the little village of Hambledon (see Walk 7) where the local cricket club had become so expert that they were able to defeat a team of the best of England's players.

Besides cricketers Hampshire also had its share of famous authors. Charles Kingsley lived at Eversley (see Walk 2) and Jane Austen spent the last 8 years of her life at Chawton (see Walk 6).

Thus Hampshire has something to interest everybody, whether they are keen on history, nature study, archaeology or just simply enjoying the splendours of the countryside. However, before setting out to explore there are a few things that must be remembered.

Firstly, parts of the county can be rather muddy. Every care has been taken in planning these walks to try and avoid the most boggy places but it is always best to wear stout waterproof footwear.

There are some areas where sheep or game birds are kept and dogs are not allowed. On the whole these places have been avoided but they do occur in Walks 12 and 29. Dogs are permitted on the routes covered by all the other walks but please remember to keep them under control and always put them on a lead in places where this is demanded, such as on the track beside the gallop in Walk 11.

Always follow the Country Code:

Guard against fire risks
Fasten all gates
Keep dogs under proper control

Keep to the paths across farmland
Avoid damaging fences, hedges and walls
Leave no litter
Safeguard water supplies
Protect wild life, wild plants and trees
Go carefully on country roads
Respect the life of the countryside.

These rules are intended to help you as much as the local landowner and by keeping them you will help to ensure your enjoyment of walking in our beautiful countryside.

The sheet number of the appropriate 1:50,000 OS map is given at the heading of each walk.

Walk 1   Waggoners Wells

4½ miles (7 km)

OS sheet 186
Start: Ludshott Common

Set right on the Hampshire–Surrey border, Waggoners Wells is one
of the most delightful areas in the county. Magnificent beech woods
surround the chain of beautiful lakes that give it its name and a wide
variety of birds are to be seen here including heron and other water
birds.

From Ludshott Common there are beautiful views across the
wooded valleys that are so very reminiscent of the area around the
Devil's Punch Bowl in neighbouring Surrey. Part of the common has
been set aside as a small nature reserve by the National Trust and is
well worth a visit.

Because of the nature of the countryside through which this walk
is set, part of it can be rather muddy and waterproof footwear is
advisable especially after rain.

Take the B3002 from Bordon travelling towards Hindhead. Follow it
through Headley Down and, just after the houses on the right end,
park in the first National Trust car park on Ludshott Common. This
is on the right just opposite a field gate on the left.

Start the walk by going through the gap in the vehicle barrier at
the rear of the car park and following the path straight ahead. This
is almost immediately crossed by another path but ignore it and carry
straight on, disregarding two others leading to the houses behind the
trees on the right.

Not far beyond this the path joins a track which comes through the
trees from the left at a point where yet another small path goes towards
the houses on the right. Follow the track straight ahead disregarding
any paths to left and right. Where the track is crossed by another still
carry straight on. The track goes down a slope and narrows into a
path. Ignore another which joins it from the right and continue into
the trees at the bottom of the slope.

Here the path meets another in a T-junction. Turn left and where
it forks take the right-hand branch leading up a slope. At the top it is
joined by another path from the left. Ignore this and go straight on
for a short distance to where it is crossed by another that leads into
the nature reserve on the left. Turn left on to this and follow it through
the reserve ignoring a grassy path which converges with it from the
right.

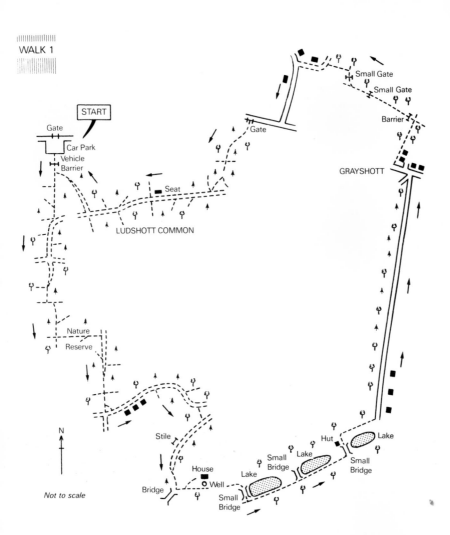

On the far side of the nature reserve the path is crossed by a track. Turn right and follow that track through the wood ignoring a path to the right in the valley and another to the left at the top of the next slope. Not far beyond this the track narrows into a path, is crossed by another and then runs on through the trees to join a track. Turn left on to this, passing a bungalow on your right.

Continue along the track until, having swung right and been joined by a path from the left, it swings left once more. At this point a path leads down a slope to the right. Turn right on to this, follow it to where it meets another track and turn right again.

13

The track can be rather muddy but it is possible to walk along the bank beside it. Ignore a stile in the fence to the right and continue to follow the track down into a valley where it swings right to cross a bridge over a stream. Leave it at this point and take a narrow path to the left which follows the stream on the right.

Disregard a path leading up to a house on the left and go straight on past the wishing well. Beyond the house the path swings right to pass a National Trust collection pillar on the left. It continues to follow the bank of the stream to the head of the first lake and then swings right across a small stone bridge.

Go over this bridge and follow the path to the far side of the lake where it joins another in a T-junction. Turn left and follow the path along beside the lake and the stream beyond. Ignore a path which crosses a small bridge to the left and carry straight on until you come to the head of the third lake. Here there is another little bridge across the stream. Turn left on to it and pass a small building on the left to reach the far side of the lake. Turn right and follow a path skirting the lake to reach a lane.

Turn left and follow the lane to where it joins the main road then cross over and turn left again. This will take you across a small side road called Waggoners Way just beyond which a path signposted 'Footpath to Whitmoor Vale' leads away to the right. Follow this to where it is crossed by another at the top of a steep slope and then turn left. The path goes through a barrier and then skirts the edge of a wood on the right. At the far side of the field it passes through a small gate in the fence and not far beyond this there is a second gate to the right. Go through it and turn sharp left ignoring a signposted footpath which leads straight ahead.

When you come to a track carry straight on to reach the lane and then turn left. This will bring you to where the lane joins the road. Turn right to follow the verge for about 100 yards and then cross over to take a path labelled 'Bridleway' which runs between two wooden fences.

Where the fence on the right ends the path is crossed by a second. Ignore this and carry straight on for a short distance to where it divides. Take the right-hand fork going through the trees to join a track. Turn right on to this, ignoring a second path that joins the track from the right and two more on the left. The track will bring you to where another path crosses it at a point where there is a seat on the right.

Still carry straight on, disregarding two more paths to the right and one to the left, until you reach a place where there is a track to the right and a path to the left. Turn right on to the track and follow it to where it narrows and is crossed by a path. Turn right here to reach the car park.

3 miles (4.5 km)

OS sheet 186
Start: Bramshill Common Wood car park

The small village of Eversley was the home of Charles Kingsley, author of *The Water Babies*. He was rector here from 1842 until his death in 1875 and his body lies in the churchyard of the church which he served.

The area to the west of Eversley is densely wooded and parts of this walk run through the plantations that cover Warren Heath which were once part of the land belonging to Bramshill House. It was near here, in 1621, that Abbot, Archbishop of Canterbury, accidentally shot a keeper whilst hunting in the park.

Take the A33 from Basingstoke travelling towards Reading and after 8 miles turn right opposite the Wellington Memorial on to a road signposted 'Heckfield 1 – Bramshill 2 – Eversley 4'. Go straight ahead at the crossroads and where the road swings right take the side road leading straight ahead and signposted 'Bramshill Police College (Heavy Vehicles)'. Follow this for about 3 miles to where some over-head electricity cables cross the road to pass under another line on the right. Turn left here into the car park marked 'Bramshill Forest, Bramshill Common Wood'.

Cross the road and follow the lane for about ten yards. Having passed under the power lines turn left on to a path skirting the pine trees on the left. The path curves to the left into the trees and eventually comes to a place where five paths meet. Take the path that leads to the right. The path goes down into a dip where it is crossed by another narrower one. Ignore this and carry straight on to the top of the next slope. Here another path leads to the left but disregard it and go straight on.

The path has now become a track and emerges into a clearing. Turn left to cross the clearing, passing another track on the left, and take a narrow path through the trees. It descends a slight slope at the bottom of which it is joined by two paths from the right. Ignore both of these and go on to where the path ends at a place where two tracks join and are met by another path from the left.

Cross the first track and turn right on to the second, keeping the fields on your left. Where the track swings right take the grassy track leading straight ahead. This soon degenerates into a path and is joined

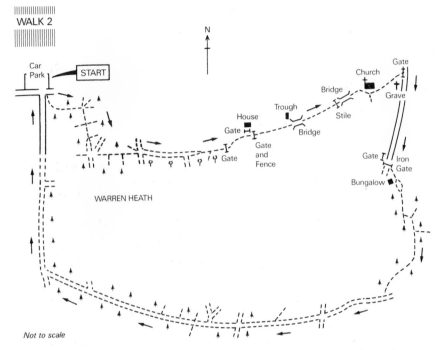

by another from the right. Ignore this and carry on to go through a gate leading into a field.

Skirt the hedge on the left. This will lead you past a gate on the left marked 'Private' to another gate in the corner of the field. Cross the three-bar fence beside this and head straight across the field towards a hedge which separates the two fields beyond. Pass to the right of a water trough to cross a small plank bridge and then follow the hedge which is now on your right.

In the far corner of the field there is a stile with a narrow path beyond. This leads over a small bridge to the churchyard. Turn right to pass the church on your left and follow the metalled path straight ahead ignoring a branch to the right opposite the church porch. Just as the ornamental trees begin to line the path a narrow turning to the right leads to Charles Kingsley's grave.

Carry on along the main path to the churchyard gate and turn right to follow the lane. Go through the iron gates at the end and immediately left on to a footpath leading through the trees. Beside the bungalow on the right it forks but take either branch for they quickly rejoin.

The path climbs a slope and branches again. Take the left-hand fork which swings left and then right and is joined by another path from the left. Disregard this and keep to the main path, ignoring another minor path to the left. When the path emerges on to an open area planted with young trees bear right to keep the mature trees on your right and the young ones on your left. This will eventually lead you across a ditch to a track.

Turn right and follow the track, ignoring another track that crosses it and a path to the right, until you reach the place where it enters the mature trees. Here it is crossed by a second track running parallel to the edge of the wood. Cross this and go straight on for a short distance. Disregard a path to the right and where the track bends right leave it to take another leading straight ahead.

Keep to this track ignoring all side turnings until, having narrowed to a wide path, it forks. Take the left-hand branch which leads straight ahead and eventually joins a gravel track. Turn right here to follow the track. It joins the head of a lane that leads down to the road and the car park.

3 miles (4.5 km)

OS sheet 186
Start: Barley Mow Bridge

The Basingstoke Canal was built during the latter half of the eighteenth century when canal boats were one of most popular methods of transporting merchandise. It was designed to carry timber, malt and flour to London and coal, groceries, china and drapery back into Hampshire, but never proved a very successful project. This was partly due to the fact that it did not connect up with any of the country's more important canals and partly to the fierce competition provided by road and sea transport.

The canal limped its way through the first two decades of the nineteenth century as a marginally profitable concern but its fate was sealed by the railway from London which was built in the 1830's. It gained a short respite in the years immediately after 1854 when large quantities of building materials were shipped along it for the construction of Aldershot Camp, but by the end of the century all traffic on it had ceased. A last attempt to reopen it was made during World War I when the army took control of the eastern end to shift government stores and munitions, but that was of short duration. During the twentieth century it lay deserted and forgotten until the Surrey and Hampshire Canal Society was formed in 1966. Due to their persuasion Surrey and Hampshire County Councils purchased the canal in 1974 and since then a great amount of restoration work has been done upon it. Much of this work can be seen on the very attractive stretch of the waterway which runs through Winchfield and Dogmersfield. Here the canal has been dredged, the tow-path cleared and bridges rebuilt.

There is a particularly large number of bridges in this area; a fact bearing witness to the canal builders' obligation to make concessions to local needs. Some of these bridges, such as Sprats Hatch Bridge, were built to serve hamlets, many of which were already rapidly disappearing as the local landowners extended their parks. Others, such as Stacey Bridge and Baseley Bridge, were built to connect farmland and were named after the farmers who were working the land at that time.

The canal makes a large loop to the north to avoid a park that was once the property of Sir Henry St John. In this park lies Tundry Pond across which the canal builders were asked to build a bridge to allow carriages to pass to the Great House. A small village once stood on

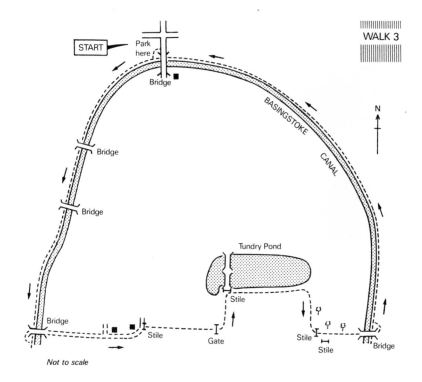

START

Park
here

Bridge

Bridge

Bridge

Bridge

BASINGSTOKE CANAL

N

Tundry Pond

Stile

Stile

Gate

Stile

Stile

Bridge

Not to scale

the banks of the pond but this was removed by the landowner when the park was landscaped.

Dogmersfield House stands on the site of a medieval Bishop's Palace and has been rebuilt several times. It was here that Prince Arthur, the eldest son of King Henry VII, first met his bride, Katherine of Aragon. Prince Arthur died just five months after the wedding and Katherine later became the first wife of his younger brother, Henry VIII.

After the Reformation Dogmersfield passed from the church into the hands of the Wriothesley family who replaced the house by a larger mansion during the reign of Elizabeth I. This was demolished in the early eighteenth century to make way for the present building.

On the banks of the canal to the east of Tundry Pond are some old wartime defences. These consist of pill boxes and heavy brick and concrete blocks, hastily erected in July 1940 when the threatened invasion seemed imminent.

Take the A323 from Hartley Wintney travelling towards Fleet. Follow it for 1½ miles and, having passed under the bridge carrying the motorway, turn right on to the road marked 'Winchfield 1 – Dogmersfield 2'. This road passes Winchfield Hospital on the left to reach a crossroads with the Barley Mow public house on the right. Go straight across on to the 'no through road' and park on the right just before the bridge.

Walk down the bank to the tow-path and turn right. This will lead you under Stacey's Bridge and Baseley's Bridge to Sprats Hatch Bridge. Go under Sprats Hatch Bridge and turn right to take a narrow path leading up to a track. Turn right to cross the bridge and follow the track to where it swings left and joins the head of a lane. Turn right again at this point to cross a stile and walk to the far side of the field.

Leave the field by a barbed-wire gate in the right-hand corner and turn left to skirt the next field, keeping the fence on your left. This will bring you to a stile in the corner of the field which gives access to the bridge across Tundry Pond. Do not cross the stile but turn right beside it to continue along the edge of the field with the pond on your left. From this point there are good views of Dogmersfield House, which stands on the far side of some fields to the right.

At the far corner of the field turn right and walk to the end of the wood on the left. Here there is another stile. Turn left to cross it and follow the path to the bridge ignoring another stile on the right.

Cross the bridge and turn sharp left to take a path leading down to the canal bank, then turn right to follow the tow-path. It is here that the old wartime fortifications can be seen on either side of the canal.

Continue along the tow-path and leave it at the next bridge, where you left the car.

Walk 4   Odiham and Greywell

$3\frac{1}{2}$ **miles (5.5 km)**

OS sheet 186
Start: Odiham church

Odiham is one of the most interesting and picturesque of the small Hampshire towns. Many of the houses in the wide main street date from the eighteenth and early nineteenth centuries and the church is the biggest in the northern part of Hampshire. Its tower of red brick was built during the Civil War and beside the churchyard wall the stocks and whipping post are to be seen.

To the north of Odiham the Basingstoke Canal winds its way towards North Warnborough and Greywell. This is one of the most interesting stretches of the canal and one that has recently undergone a great deal of restoration work. Just west of North Warnborough is a swing bridge which is still fully functional and can be raised in just one and a half minutes.

At Greywell the canal enters a tunnel which carries it for 1,230 yards through the hillside. The tunnel was built in 1792 but no provision was made for a tow-path. When the canal came into use the horses, which had pulled the boats all the way from London, were unhitched and led over the hill whilst the bargees lay on their backs on the barge and forced the vessel through the tunnel by pushing against the wall with their feet.

Beside the canal between North Warnborough and Greywell stand the remains of King John's Castle. This was built during the first decade of the thirteenth century at the order of King John who used it as a hunting lodge and a place at which to break his journeys between Windsor and Winchester. It was from this castle that the king rode to Runnymede in 1215 to set his seal on the Magna Carta. During the following year the castle was besieged by Louis, Dauphin of France, and in the fourteenth century it was the prison of King David of Scotland.

Once King John's Castle was an impressive place but now little remains except the ruins of the octagonal keep. Parts of the outer bailey were destroyed during the eighteenth century when the canal was cut through it and the surrounding moat.

Leave the M3 at junction 5 and take the A287, signposted 'Farnham'. This will bring you into Odiham. After the road swings left into the main street at a point where the A32 to Alton goes straight ahead, take the first turning on the right. This is signposted 'Car Park –

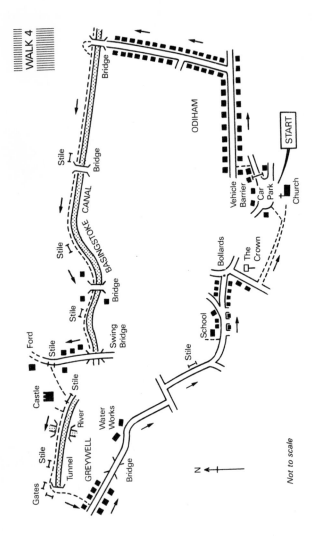

WALK 4

ODIHAM

START

Church

Car Park

Vehicle Barrier

The Crown

Bollards

School

Stile

Bridge

BASINGSTOKE CANAL

Stile

Stile

Stile

Bridge

Stile

Ford

Swing Bridge

Castle

Stile

River

Water Works

GREYWELL

Tunnel

Stile

Gates

Bridge

N

Not to scale

Parish Church'. When you reach the place where the road widens park in the parking spaces beside the churchyard wall.

Walk away from the churchyard and to the right to reach a narrow lane which goes through a vehicle barrier passing Bury Cottage on the left. Pass one other cottage on the left beyond the barrier and then turn left on to a footpath which leads down to the main road. Go across the pedestrian crossing and turn right to follow the main road through the town. This will bring you to a road on the left marked 'A30 London – Staines'. Turn left and follow this road to where it crosses a bridge over the canal.

On the far side of the bridge turn left on to a path which leads down to the canal, then follow the tow-path straight ahead. Pass a bridge that gives access to the fields on the far side of the canal and two stiles on the right and follow the canal under another bridge. Beyond this there is another stile on the right but disregard it and continue along the tow-path until you reach the swing bridge which has been recently renovated. Turn right here to follow the lane and just before the ford turn left to cross a stile marked 'Footpath'.

Walk straight across the field to another stile at the far side. This will give you a good view of King John's Castle on the right. Cross the stile and turn right to follow the tow-path once more. It will lead you past King John's Castle on the right to where the river Whitewater passes under the canal. This was originally achieved by channelling the river water through wooden pipes laid under the bed of the canal and it worked very well. When these pipes were replaced in 1975 they were still in a good state of preservation in spite of having been in use for 200 years.

Continue along the tow-path to the mouth of the Greywell Tunnel ignoring another stile on the right. Follow the path up the slope beside the tunnel mouth and then turn left to pass across the top of it. From here a narrow path leads between gardens to the road. Turn left and follow the road out of Greywell village. Having passed the waterworks on the left it climbs a slope to meet another road in a T-junction. Turn left and then right on to a road signposted 'South Warnborough 2½'.

Disregard a stile in the fence to the left and follow the road round to the left. This will lead you past the secondary school on your left. Not far beyond this the road swings sharp left again. Cross over at this point and take the 'no through road' which goes straight ahead passing a house called West Croft on your right. This will lead you through some bollards to the main road.

Turn right on to the road to Alton and, having passed a public house called The Crown on your left, turn left into a narrow lane leading to the churchyard. At the edge of the churchyard the lane becomes a path which almost immediately forks. Take the left-hand branch leading back to the road where you left the car.

Museum Tu to Sun & Bank Holiday Mondays
12:00 - 5:30 pm.

Walk 5   Selborne

3 miles (4.5 km)

OS sheet 186
Start: The car park behind the Selborne Arms

The attractive little village of Selborne, nestling beneath its high tree-clad hanger, was once the home of the famous naturalist Gilbert White. It is set in one of the most beautiful parts of Hampshire; a place abounding with a wide variety of flora and fauna including many rare species.

Gilbert White was born in the village in 1720 and lived there in The Wakes, the old family home, from 1729 until his death in 1793. He was a curate by profession but his consuming interest always lay in the natural history of the area in which he lived. It was at The Wakes that he wrote *The Natural History and Antiquities of Selborne* – a book that served to make both the author and his village famous.

Today The Wakes is a museum owned by The Oates Memorial Trust. Its lower rooms are devoted to a collection of relics and information relating to the naturalist whilst on the upper floor are items connected with the life of Captain Oates who died with Scott on his ill-fated expedition to the South Pole in 1912.

The zigzag winding its way up the steep face of Selborne Hanger was cut out by Gilbert White and his brother in 1753 to serve as a short cut to the top of this high chalk hill. From the summit there is a marvellous view and to the left of the path at this point is a lump of rock, commonly known as the Wishing Stone, which was brought here from Farringdon by Gilbert White and his brothers.

The open space dividing the churchyard from the main road is called the Plestor. This is an old-fashioned word meaning a play place or a village green. Here the stocks and whipping post used to stand but they were so unpopular that they were secretly removed by one of the villagers in 1750 and, in spite of a reward being offered for their return, were never recovered.

The church dates back to 1180 and was built on the site of an earlier Saxon one. Just inside the churchyard is a giant yew tree believed to be over 1,000 years old and one of the biggest in the country. Beneath its branches stands a short stone pillar marking the Trumpeter's Grave. The Trumpeter was a man named Newland who lived in the village during the nineteenth century. He gained notoriety during a riot which took place there in 1830 by blowing a horn to encourage the mob of villagers who were protesting against church taxes.

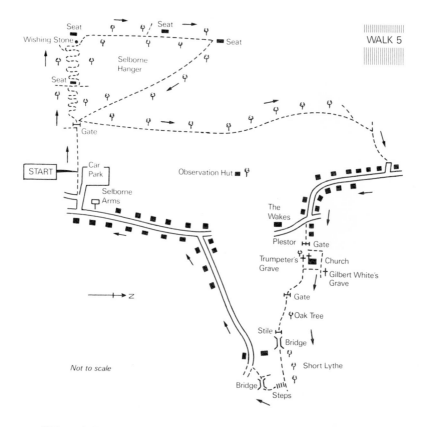

Gilbert White's grave, situated on the north side of the church, is very simple. Its low headstone is marked merely with his initials and the date of his death.

Turn off the A31 on to the B3006 at Alton and follow the signs to Selborne. Having entered the village turn right just beyond the Selborne Arms and park in the public car park at the rear of the building.

Leave the car park by the footpath which leads to the zigzag. This will bring you to a small gate in the fence at the edge of Selborne Common. Ignore a footpath curving away to the left at this point and go through the gate. Turn left to pass the National Trust sign on your right and climb the zigzag.

Disregard a path crossing the zigzag at right-angles about half way up at a point where there is a seat and continue to climb. Near the top the path forks. Keep to the right-hand branch which will lead you to where the Wishing Stone and another seat are on your left. This is the view point at the top of the zigzag and it is worth pausing here to enjoy the beautiful view of the valley.

Leave the view point by the way you entered it passing the Wishing Stone on your right and take the path which leads straight ahead through the trees. Ignore any side turnings and keep the downward slope of the hanger on your right. Slowly the path widens and, after a short distance, appears to fork. The left-hand branch quickly swings round to climb higher up the hillside so keep to the right which will almost immediately lead you past a wooden seat.

About 200 yards beyond this there is another seat, this time a metal one, sited slightly down the slope to the right. From this seat there is a good view of The Wakes in the valley straight ahead.

Turn sharp right here on to a path leading down the hillside and passing the seat on your left. This will bring you back to the National Trust sign at the foot of the zigzag. Turn sharp left on to a path which skirts the fence on the right. Almost immediately the wooden fence gives way to a wire one and at this point a reconstruction of Gilbert White's observation hut can be seen, surrounded by a protective fence, in the middle of the field to the right.

Further along the path passes the rear of The Wakes, beyond the field on the right, and then continues to follow the fence until it eventually joins a wider path from the left at the far end of the hanger. Turn right on to this and follow it down a slight slope passing a National Trust sign on the left to where it joins another path in a T-junction. Turn right again and walk along this path which leads between high banks to the head of a lane. Go down the lane to the T-junction and turn right into another lane. This will eventually lead you back to the B3006.

Cross the road and take the path that goes straight ahead, passing the Plestor on the right and The Old Vicarage on the left, to reach the gate that gives access to the churchyard. Turn left to pass the yew tree and Trumpeter's Grave on your right and take the path leading round behind the church.

Follow the path along the northern side of the church to where it leaves the wall beside a section of low roof on the right; Gilbert White's grave is to the left of the path directly opposite this.

Carry on along the path which swings right to skirt the end of the church ignoring another which leads straight ahead. Where the path joins a wider one turn left and follow this to the far corner of the churchyard. Here a gate in the hedge gives access to a field. Go through the gate and straight down the slope passing an oak tree on your left to reach a stile at the far end of the field. Cross the stile and the bridge beyond and follow the path straight ahead through the Short Lythe.

Having passed the cottage on your right and followed the stream for a short distance, the path is joined by another which comes up some steps from the right. Turn on to this and follow it along beside the fence on the left to a bridge. Turn right to cross the bridge and, ignoring a path to the right, take the one straight ahead leading up to where a track meets the end of a lane.

Turn right to follow the lane back to the road and then left to return to the Selborne Arms and the car park.

Walk 6   Chawton Park Wood

3 miles (4.5 km)

OS sheet 186
Start: Chawton Park Wood car park

This beautiful wooded area lies to the west of Alton. It is named after the near-by village of Chawton where Jane Austen spent the last eight years of her life. She died in 1817 at the early age of 41, just a few months before her last novel *Persuasion* was published.

Throughout her life Jane Austen was a keen walker and during her time at Chawton she was a frequent visitor to the neighbouring Chawton Park Woods. In those days these woods were composed mainly of beautiful beech trees but now many of these are gone, their place being taken by stands of fir and larch trees planted by the Forestry Commission.

Take the A31 from Alton to Four Marks and turn right just beyond Chawton End Garage on to a road signposted 'Medstead 1½'. Follow this road to where it swings sharp left then take a track straight ahead. Chawton Park Wood car park is on the right.

Leave the car park by the gap at the far end and turn right. Walk towards the water tower and then left on to a track which skirts the trees on the left and has a hedge on the right. Follow this for some distance ignoring a track which goes through a vehicle barrier on the right and another two grassy tracks leading into the trees on the left. Beyond the second of these the track swings slightly left and then runs past a pond at the edge of the trees. The pond is very small with brackish water but at the right time of the year its surface is gay with water plants.

Not far beyond the pond the track goes through a gap in a fence at a point where there is a small gate to the right and a path to the left. Ignore both of these and follow the track straight ahead to where it meets another in a T-junction. Turn left and walk past some buildings on the left to reach a vehicle barrier.

Beyond the vehicle barrier the track becomes a wide grassy ride which leads through the trees to a clearing. Go straight ahead, ignoring a track to the right, to reach a point where another track leads down a steep slope. From the top of this slope there is a good view across the wood which covers the valley and the hillside beyond. Descend the slope and turn left on to the track running through the valley. This is almost immediately joined by a path from the left, but ignore this and carry straight on.

28

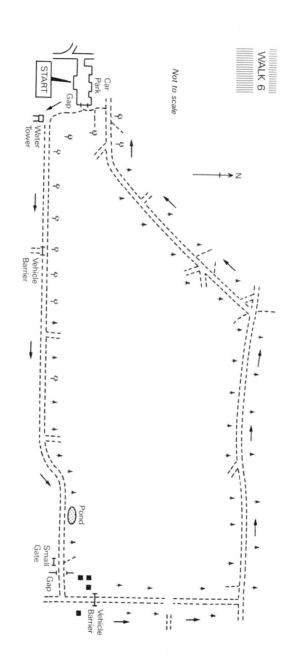

WALK 6

Not to scale

N

START

Car
Park

Gap

Water
Tower

Vehicle
Barrier

Pond

Small
Gate

Gap

Vehicle
Barrier

Pass a track on the left and when you come to a second turn left. Keep to this track ignoring all side turnings until you eventually reach a place where a sign to the right of the track indicates the beginnings of the forest walk and the forest trail. Turn left opposite this and, ignoring a path leading into the trees on the left, head towards the water tower. After about 50 yards the car park is on your right.

Walk 7   Hambledon – The Home of Cricket

6 miles (9.5 km)

OS sheets 185 and 196
Start: Hambledon village

This is a pleasant walk through rolling downland scenery but parts of it can be rather wet, especially when the crops are high, so it is advisable to wear waterproof footwear.

The village of Hambledon nestles amongst the high chalk hills to the north of Portsmouth where the western tip of the South Downs stretches into Hampshire. It is the largest village in the area and also one of the oldest.

Hambledon's main claim to fame was its cricket club. This was formed during the latter half of the eighteenth century and made a name for itself when it challenged and defeated an All-England team in 1770. The club was founded by the Rev. Charles Pawlett and one of its members, Richard Nyren, was the author of *The Young Cricketer's Guide and The Cricketers of My Time* – a book still considered to be one of the greatest literary works on cricket.

Hambledon Cricket Club played on Broadhalfpenny Down to the north-east of the village. Here a granite monument marks the site of the original pitch. The monument was unveiled in 1908 when a crowd of 5,000 people came to watch the first match to be played on the site after an interval of a hundred years.

Take the A3 from Portsmouth travelling towards Petersfield and turn left in Waterlooville on to the road to Denmead. This is Hambledon Road. Follow it through Denmead to Hambledon and turn right on to the road marked 'Village Centre ¼ – Broadhalfpenny Down 2½'. Park on the left-hand side of this road beyond the Vine Inn.

Begin the walk by going along the village street and turning right beside the George Hotel. This will bring you into a narrow lane which runs up a hill. Ignore a footpath to the right opposite Hill House and continue to follow the lane. At the top of the hill it is joined by a narrow lane from the left and a track marked 'Footpath' which leads straight ahead. Disregard both of these and follow the lane round to the right.

Not far beyond Rushmere Arabian Stud there is a road junction. Turn left here and follow the lane until you come to a track on the left marked 'Footpath'. Turn left on to this. The track curves right to pass the edge of a wood on the right. At this point it is joined by another, rather overgrown track which skirts the trees. Disregard this and carry

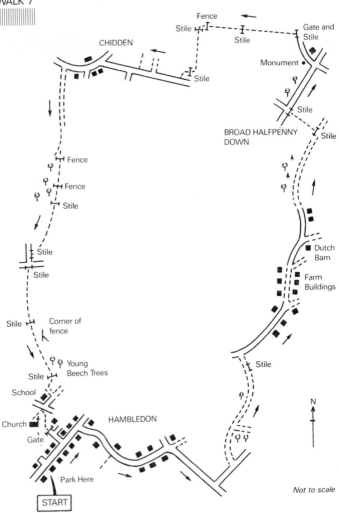

straight on. The track swings left again and passes a stile set in the fence on the right. Ignore this and go on to where the track meets a lane.

Turn right and walk along the lane passing some farm buildings and a track on the right. Just beyond this the lane degenerates into a track and leads through a farmyard. Go straight ahead ignoring a track to the right.

Beyond the farmyard the track widens into a lane once more. Disregard an unmetalled lane which joins it from the right by a Dutch barn and go on to pass some more farm buildings and a house on the right. Just after these the lane becomes an unmetalled track. It runs between hedges for some distance before emerging to pass a plantation of young trees on the left and descend a slope. Near the bottom there is a stile in the fence on the left. Cross this and walk down the hillside to leave the field by another stile which gives access to the road.

Turn right to walk up the hill to the crossroads and turn left. This will lead you past the cricket pitch and the monument on the left.

Continue to follow the road for about another 100 yards and then turn left to cross a stile beside a field gate. Walk along the side of the field keeping the fence on your left and cross a second stile at the far side of the field. Carry straight on, still keeping the fence on the left. This will bring you to a three-bar fence in the corner of the field. Cross this and turn left almost immediately to climb another stile and follow the fence on the right.

Near the far corner of the field turn right across a stile to reach a lane. Turn right to follow the lane which goes down a slope and is joined by a track from the right. Ignore this and a footpath on the right at the top of the next slope. Just beyond the footpath the lane is joined by another lane from the left marked 'no through road'. Ignore it and carry on to where the lane merges with another from the right. Go round the bend to the left. This is signposted 'Hambledon 2¼'.

At the next junction bear right on to the road signposted 'Meonstoke 3¼ – Droxford 3¾'. Follow the lane up a slope for about 75 yards and then turn left on to a track leading between fields with a hedge on the left.

After some distance the track becomes a path which runs between bushes and then turns slightly right into a wood. Leave it at this point to cross a two-bar fence straight ahead and then keep the edge of the wood on your right. This will lead you through a gap in a barbed-wire fence and over a stile to where the wood on the right ends. Bear slightly right to reach the far corner of the field. Here a second stile enables you to reach a metalled track.

Turn left to follow the track to the road. Cross it and go over a stile on the far side to carry on up the slope keeping the hedge on your left. This will lead you over the brow of the hill to a stile at the far corner of the field. Cross this and go slightly right to pass the corner of a fence on your left.

Follow the narrow grassy path which heads obliquely right down the hillside towards the school in the valley and leads past a clump of young beech trees on the left to a stile at the lower edge of the field. Go over this and turn right, then follow the narrow path between allotments to a track. Turn left and walk past the school on your right to where the track meets a metalled one at right-angles. Turn right and follow the metalled track to the lane beyond the school.

Cross over and turn left to take the path through the churchyard passing the church on your right. This will bring you to a gateway beyond which is a lane. Walk straight down the lane to the road where you parked the car.

Walk 8   Silchester

5 miles (8 km)

OS sheet 175
Start: Kings Road, Silchester

To the east of Silchester lie buried some of the most interesting Roman
remains to be found in England. There, beneath the fields, is what is
left of the Roman city of Calleva. Today, little can be seen except the
old city wall and the overgrown remains of an amphitheatre once
capable of holding 10,000 spectators.

The Roman city was built on a site that was originally fortified by
the Celts. It was an extensive township covering some 235 acres and
included amongst its buildings the oldest known Christian church in
England.

The sites occupied by most Roman cities have developed into
modern townships but Calleva did not and in this it is almost unique.
Nobody knows quite why it died. It might have been merely because
it failed to serve any useful purpose once the Romans had left or it
may have been due to some more dramatic cause such as plague.

On the eastern border of the Roman site and well away from the
main complex of houses which form the village of Silchester, stands
the present Silchester church. Dating from the thirteenth century it
contains a fine Jacobean pulpit and some interesting wall paintings
from around the time when the church was built.

Calleva means 'the town in the wood' and in Roman times it was
surrounded by thick woodland which stretched westward from Kent.
Today little of this remains but to the north of the village there is an
area of pleasant woodland known as Benyon's Inclosure. It is bordered
to the east by Mortimer West End, a small hamlet that lies right on
the county boundary.

Take the A340 from Basingstoke travelling towards Aldermaston and
turn right in Pamber Green on to the road to Little London. Where
this ends in a T-junction turn left following the signpost 'Silchester
$1\frac{3}{4}$'. This will bring you to the Calleva Arms on the left. Turn left here
and pass the cricket ground on your right. Take the first road on the
right and follow it for about 100 yards before turning left to park
beside the beginning of a gravel track to the left of a pair of cottages
called Heatherbrae and Firgate.

Cross the stile beside the vehicle barrier and follow the track,
ignoring a grassy track to the right near the edge of the trees. Continue
along the track, disregarding a path to the left and two more tracks

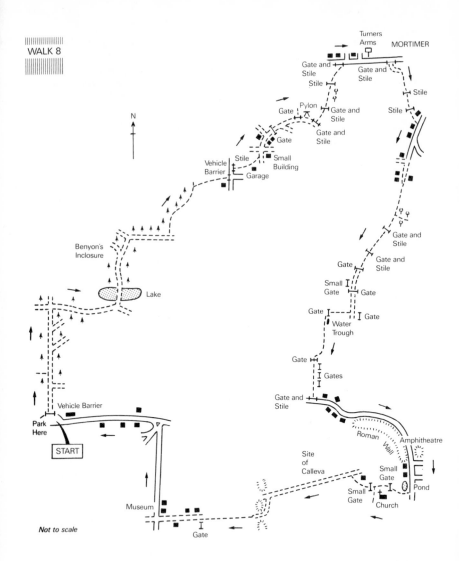

Not to scale

to the right until you reach a place where the track is crossed by another.

Turn right here and walk along the track to where, after emerging from the trees, it forks. Take the left-hand branch. This crosses a lake and then climbs a slope and turns left. At this point a narrower track leads straight ahead. Turn off the main track on to this and where it meets a second track in a T-junction turn right. Continue along this track until the wood on the left comes to an end and then turn left on to a path which runs through the edge of the trees skirting some fields on the right.

The path leads down a slope and crosses a small stream beyond which it forks. Take the right-hand branch. This climbs a slope and passes a house on the right before going through a vehicle barrier to join the road. Cross over and turn left to follow the verge to the first telegraph pole, then turn right over a stile into a field. Follow the hedge on the right which curves slightly left and, having passed a garage on your right, head straight across the field towards a small building on the far side.

This will bring you to a gravel track. Turn left and, ignoring a track which crosses the one you are following, carry straight on. The track passes some farm buildings on the right and meets another track in a T-junction. Turn right, passing the farmhouse on your right, and follow the track through a metal gate. Just beyond it the track divides. Keep to the left-hand fork.

Ignore a path which leads through a gate to the left just before the electricity pylons and carry on along the track to turn left over a stile beside the next gate on the left. Go straight ahead to cross another stile beside a second gate and then follow the path that skirts the wood on the right. At the top of the slope is another stile. Cross it and carry straight on, keeping the fence on your right until you come to a gate and a stile giving access to the road.

Cross the road and turn right. This will lead you past the Turners Arms on the left. Having passed it continue along the pavement for about another 60 yards and then re-cross the road to climb over a stile beside a metal gate on to a track.

Follow the track round to the left through some bushes and, where it ends, turn right to skirt the edge of the field, keeping the hedge on your right. Where the hedge curves near the corner of the field is another stile. Cross this and carry on with the hedge on your left to reach a third stile beyond which a path leads between some houses to the road.

Turn right and follow the road to where it forks. Take the right-hand branch, labelled 'Simms Stud Farm' and, where the tarmac ends, continue to go straight ahead ignoring a track to the right. Having passed some farm buildings on the right and a house on the left the track degenerates into a path. Where it forks keep to the right-hand branch going down a slope to a gate with a stile beside it. Cross the stile and walk over the field to another gate with a stile beside it. Beyond this is a narrow path.

Go through the gate at the end of the path and follow the track straight ahead, ignoring a small gate on the right, to reach a third which bars the track. Go through this and continue along the track until you reach another gate in the fence on the left. Turn right beside this gate to cross the field and go through another on the far side. Then turn left to pass a water trough on the left and follow the fence. This will bring you to a wooden gate in the far corner of the field. Go through it and, ignoring three gates on the left, walk straight ahead to reach a gate with a stile beside and the road beyond.

Turn left to follow the road. It will lead you past parts of the Roman wall on your right and, just before it is joined by another road from the left, the amphitheatre is on the left. Unfortunately this is now covered by trees and without careful inspection it is difficult to discern its original shape.

Ignore the road to the left just beyond the amphitheatre and another which comes from the left a little further on and continue along the road to where the church of St Mary the Virgin is set back from the road on the right.

Turn right at this point and bear right through the church car park, passing the pond on your right. This will bring you to a gate on the left that leads into the churchyard. Go through it and follow the path, ignoring a turning to the left at the far end of the church, to another small gate on the opposite side of the churchyard. Beyond this is a path leading to a track.

Turn left and follow the track. It runs straight across the centre of what was once Calleva. A good idea of the size of the city can be gained from this track as the Roman walls which marked its boundary can be seen across the fields on either side.

Where the track divides at the far side of the city site take the left-hand fork. This curves left to follow the course of the city wall on the right for a short distance and then swings right to cut through a gap in it.

Beyond this the track becomes a path and skirts a field on the right before passing through a gap beside a wooden gate to join the head of an unmetalled lane. Follow this to the road and turn right to pass the Calleva museum on your right. This will bring you to a road junction. Cross over and take the road signposted 'Pamber Heath'. This is Kings Road and the place where you left the car is a few hundred yards along it on the right.

Walk 9   Cheriton

4½ miles (7 km)

OS sheet 185
Start: Cheriton village

On several occasions Cheriton has won the annual award for the best
kept village in Hampshire and it is certainly one of the most beautiful. It
is situated on the banks of a small stream which is the beginning of the
river Itchen. This rises in the hills not far south of the village and flows
through Winchester and Eastleigh to join the sea at Southampton.

Cheriton Mill, which stands beside the stream just north of the
village, is an old water-mill. It has not been used for many years but
the mill-race that once drove the water-wheel is still visible. It runs
through an arch beneath the mill and emerges beside the footpath.

It was on the hills above Cheriton that one of the most important
battles of the Civil War was fought. On 28 March 1644 Lord Hopton
marched the Royalist army from Winchester to intercept the Round-
heads who had been led into Hampshire by Sir William Waller. They
met close to Cheriton Wood which Waller immediately occupied
whilst Hopton did his best to dislodge him. The armies were well
matched, having almost 10,000 men apiece, and the encounter lasted
for several hours. It resulted in the Royalists being badly beaten and
the slaughter was so great that the lanes are said to have run with
blood.

The Battle of Cheriton marked a turning point in the war. It was
a defeat from which the Royalist army never recovered and which
ultimately led to the downfall of King Charles I.

Take the B3046 from New Alresford to Cheriton and drive through
the village to turn left at the war memorial. Park on the left by the
village green.

Walk on along the lane and bear left into a narrower one marked
'no entry'. This will lead you up to the main road. Cross over and
take the lane straight ahead, marked 'no through road'. Follow it for
about 50 yards to pass a green barn on the right and then turn right
across a stile on to a grassy footpath. The footpath runs along beside
a hedge on the right to a gate with a stile beside it. Cross this and
continue to follow the hedge.

Within a short distance there is a gate in the hedge but ignore this
and carry straight on. The path, which had become rather indistinct,
is now clearly visible again and the hedge on the right gives way to a
fence with the narrow river Itchen beyond.

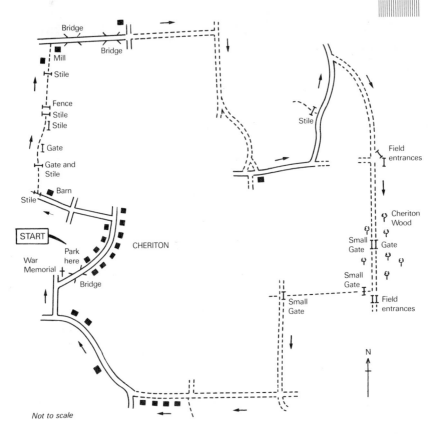

Not to scale

Disregard a stile in the fence and go straight ahead to reach one at the far end of the field. Cross this and the section of fence just beyond it and head for the white fence at the other side of the field. Here there is another stile giving access to a grassy path. It will lead you down to the lane passing a cottage on the left and Cheriton Mill on the right.

Turn right to follow the lane up to the road and cross over to take the track straight ahead. It leads up a slope and meets a second track in a T-junction. Turn right on to this track. Follow it to where it widens and divides, then take the left-hand fork. This will eventually bring you to a lane. Turn left to follow it. Where it swings left a track leads straight ahead but disregard this and continue along the lane. Ignore a footpath which begins at a stile on the left and carry straight on to reach a second track on the right.

Turn on to this and follow it up the slope. At the top it is joined by another track from the right but ignore it and carry straight on.

You are now in the area where the battle was fought in 1644. The track dips down to skirt Cheriton Wood on the left and just as it enters the trees it begins to climb again. Ignore a gate on the left marked 'Private no admittance' and a smaller one opposite it and continue to where the track emerges from the wood.

At this point there are field entrances on either side. Just before them a narrow path leads through the bushes on the right to a small gate. Turn right and go through the gate, then continue straight ahead, keeping the fence on your left. This will bring you to another small gate at the far side of the field. It opens on to a track with another path straight ahead.

Turn left on to the track and follow it to where four tracks meet then turn right. Continue along this track, ignoring a path leading away to the left and another track to the right just before the houses begin on the left.

From here the track becomes an unmetalled lane leading down to the road. Cross over and turn right to follow the road back to the war memorial.

Walk 10   Preston Candover

4 miles (6 km)

OS sheet 185
Start: Preston Candover

Preston Candover is one of the three villages which take their names from the little Candover brook that joins the river Itchen near Alresford. It is larger than either Chilton Candover or Brown Candover and is set amongst the rolling chalk hills of central Hampshire.

Preston House, lying to the north of the village, was built during the early eighteenth century. It was the home of William Guiddott whose family originally came from Florence during the reign of Edward VI. Guiddott died not long after the house was completed and it was inherited by his nephew William Woodruffe. Since then it has been sold several times and is now the property of the Sainsbury family.

Moundsmere Manor is an attractive house situated to the north-west of Preston Candover. It is much younger than Preston House, being less than a hundred years old, and was the home of Wilfred Buckley who was a pioneer in clean milk production.

A model dairy farm he built near the manor became quite famous in farming circles during the early part of this century.

Turn off the A31 in New Alresford on to the B3046 to Basingstoke. Follow this road for approximately 8 miles to Preston Candover and then drive on through the village to park in the lay-by on the left opposite Preston Candover Primary School.

Cross over and walk on along the road passing the primary school on your right. This will lead you out of the village. Ignore the road to Bradley on the right and carry straight on, passing Preston House on your left. Not far beyond it there is a drive on the right flanked by two gatehouses. It is marked 'Private drive' but this is only to deter motorists. Turn right and follow it up the slope from the top of which there are some good views across the hills to the right.

After this the drive leads on through a wood to the gates of Moundsmere Manor. Here it is joined by two tracks, one to the right and one to the left. Take the right-hand one. It will lead you past the manor house set back beyond a field on the left.

The track leads down into a valley and swings right at a point where it is joined by another track from the left. Ignore this and continue along the main track until you reach a point where it divides, then take the right-hand fork. This is grass covered and leads straight ahead through some bushes.

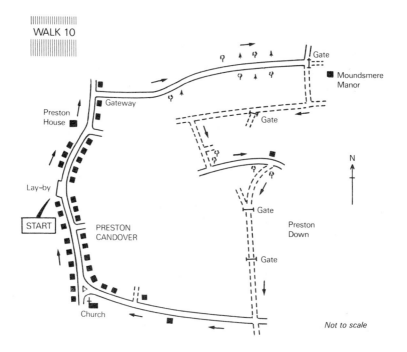

Preston House

Gateway

Preston
House

Lay-by

START

PRESTON
CANDOVER

Church

Gate

Moundsmere
Manor

Gate

Gate

Preston
Down

Gate

N

Not to scale

Follow the track to where it is joined by another track from the left and then turn left. The track climbs a slope and is joined by another track from the left near the corner of a wood. Disregard this and carry straight on passing the wood on your left to reach the place where the track meets the road. Turn left and follow the verge to where the road swings slightly right and there is a cottage on the left. Cross the road at this point and turn sharp right on to a track leading through the bushes.

The track runs for some distance between hedges and then is joined by another track from the right at a point where there is a gate straight ahead. Go through the gate and follow the track on across the field to the top of the hill. This is called the Ox Drove but it is really part of Preston Down. From here there is a good view of Preston House lying in the valley to the right.

Continue along the track which runs across the hilltop and then dips down to pass through another gate at the far side of the field. From here the track becomes more distinct. It leads between hedges with fields on either side and eventually joins a road.

Turn right to walk along the road. It will take you past Down Farm on the left and then on down a hill to Preston Candover. The road meets the main road through the village in a T-junction at a point where the church is on the left. Turn right and follow the road back through the village to the lay-by where you left the car.

Walk 11   Kingsclere and Watership Down

8 miles (12.5 km)

OS sheets 174 and 185
Start: Whitehill Viewpoint car park

The village of Kingsclere lies in the north of the county not far from the Berkshire border. It is set amongst beautiful rolling downland from the crests of which there are magnificent views. Parts of this downland are used for sheep but large sections have been set aside for training racehorses from local stables. It is on these downs that some of England's greatest winners have been trained including Ormond and Flying Fox.

In Saxon times these hills had a very different use. In those days Kingsclere was a royal manor and the hills a royal hunting ground. William the Conqueror exchanged this manor for land in Winchester on which to build a castle but the English kings still continued to hunt here. King John in particular was a frequent visitor.

Across the hills to the south of Watership Down runs a Roman road known as Portway. It comes from the old Roman town of Calleva, the remains of which are near the village of Silchester in northern Hampshire, and it leads on through Wiltshire to Old Sarum. Although large sections of it have disappeared beneath the plough parts of it are still used today.

The delightful little village of Hannington stands high on a hill to the south of Kingsclere. Parts of its fine old church date back to the twelfth century.

Leave Basingstoke on the A339 travelling towards Newbury and turn left in Kingsclere on to the B3051 which is signposted 'Overton 6'. Follow this for $1\frac{1}{2}$ miles to where Whitehill Viewpoint car park is on the left.

Walk back to the road and turn sharp left on to a track which has a field entrance to the right. The track forks almost immediately but take either branch for they both converge on a field gate. Go through the gate and straight ahead, keeping the fence on your right, to reach another gate at the top of the slope. Beyond this is a track which eventually joins a lane. The part of this lane to the right is a section of the old Roman road.

Turn left and then almost immediately right on to a lane signposted 'Walkeridge Farm'. Leave this where it turns right at the farm and go straight ahead, passing the farm buildings on your right, to reach a gate with a small gate beside it.

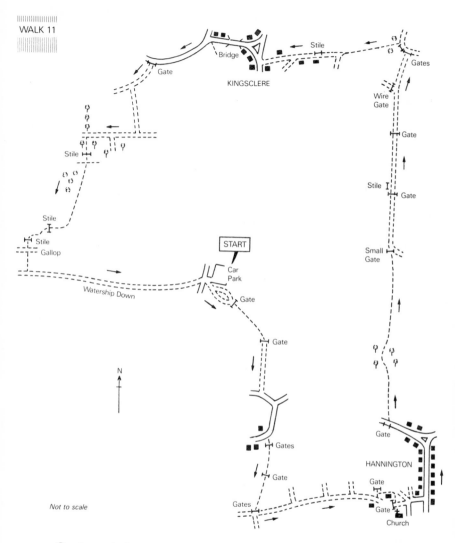

Go through the small gate and follow the fence on the left passing through two fields to reach the bottom of a slope. Here there is another gate with a small gate beside it and a track beyond. Turn left and follow it through the field. At the top of the slope it is joined by a grassy track from the left. Disregard this and carry straight on, ignoring a second track to the left part of the way up the next slope and a third at the top. Beyond this the track leads into the grounds of a house.

45

When you come to the first building on the right, turn left to walk towards a field gate. Do not go through it but turn right beside it to take a narrow path passing between the fence and a wooden building on the right. The path turns right to skirt the rear of the building and then emerges on to a drive with Hannington church straight ahead.

Turn left and walk along the drive to the road, then go straight ahead passing the village green on your right. At the far corner of the green turn left to follow the road through the village. Where it turns right by Meadham Cottage and is joined by a lane from the left, turn left to follow the lane out of the village. Not far beyond the final cottages turn right on to a path signposted 'Bridleway to Kingsclere'. The path leads across a field and through a wood and then down a slope skirting a hedge on the left.

At the top of the next slope the path goes through a small gate and joins a track. From here there are beautiful views of the Berkshire countryside to the north. Follow the track straight ahead. It goes down a slope and through a gate beyond which there is a stile on the left. Disregard the stile and continue along the track through a second gate. Ignore a track leading through a wire gate to the left and carry on to a pair of gates straight ahead.

Here the track is joined by another from the right. Turn left and then immediately left again on to a path leading through the bushes. It eventually widens into a track at a point where it is joined by another track from the left. Ignore this and a stile to the right and carry straight on to where the track forks. Take the right-hand branch. This is signposted 'Bridleway' and goes straight ahead to join the road.

Cross over and take the road signposted 'Sydmonton $2\frac{1}{2}$ – Old Burghclere $3\frac{1}{2}$'. This will bring you to a T-junction. Turn left and follow the verge for just under $\frac{1}{2}$ mile to where a grassy track signposted 'Footpath' leads through a gate to the left. Watership Down is now straight ahead of you.

The track skirts a gallop used by the horses from the racing stables so if you have a dog with you please keep it on a lead. Follow the track to where it is joined by another from the left and then turn left. This track leads across the fields and joins another in a T-junction. Turn right and follow this track. As it passes some trees on the left it is joined by another track which leads into the wood but ignore this and carry on until the track is met by a hedge from the right. At this point turn sharp left to climb a steep slope through the trees to a stile.

Cross the stile and head diagonally right up the hillside keeping the bushes on your right. It is a stiff climb but well worth it as the view from the top is magnificent. Ignore a small path running along the foot of the hill and a sunken track that leads up the hillside to the left.

Having reached the crest of the down bear right to follow the fence on the left. This eventually meets another fence at right-angles. Cross the stile in this fence and carry straight on, still following the fence on the left.

After about 75 yards you will come to a stile on the left. Cross this and go straight ahead up the bank, over the gallop and on across the grass to reach a track. Turn left and follow the track which runs along the top of Watership Down and eventually joins the road just opposite the car park.

Walk 12   Fawley Down

4 miles (6 km)

OS sheet 185
Start: The car park at Cheesefoot Head

There is very little to be said about this walk except that it is a very
pleasant one through beautiful open countryside with a variety of
good views. Unfortunately some of it runs through land used for sheep
and so dogs are not allowed.

Cheesefoot Head, where the walk begins, is just under 600 feet
high and gives magnificent, uninterrupted views to north and south.
At its northern foot lies the Devil's Punch Bowl; a much smaller
natural amphitheatre than its namesake at Hindhead but every bit
as beautiful.

Turn off the A31 just east of Winchester on to the A272 to Petersfield.
Follow this road for a little over a mile to the top of Telegraph Hill
and park in the car park on the left at Cheesefoot Head. The entrance
to this car park is just beyond the bus stop.

Leave the car park and turn right to pass the bus stop then walk on
along the verge for a short distance to reach a small gate on the right.
Do not go through the gate but cross the road at this point to take a
track marked 'Bridleway to Morestead' which leads through a field
gate on the far side. Follow this track across the field, through a second
gate (which needs to be opened with care because one of the hinges
is broken) and on along the ridge. There are some very good views
from here across the hills to the south and later towards Winchester
in the north.

At the far end of the ridge the track swings left and is joined by
another from the right. Ignore this and follow the track round to the
left. It leads down a slope skirting some army ranges on the right.

Ignore a track to the left just beyond a barn and carry on through
a short belt of trees to where there is a second track on the left marked
'Bridleway'. Turn left on to this passing a house on your right. Disregard a track to the left, but where the main track forks keep to the
left-hand branch. It leads straight ahead and down a slope to a valley
where it forks again. This time take the right-hand branch which also
goes straight ahead.

Beyond this point the track quickly degenerates into a narrow path
between hedges and leads up a slope. Near the top the hedge on the
right gives way to a fence and that on the left becomes much lower so
that, for a short distance, the panoramic views can be enjoyed once

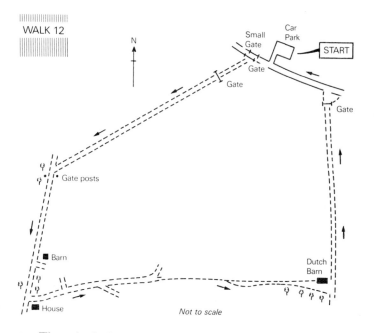

WALK 12

N

Car Park

Small Gate

START

Gate

Gate

Gate

Gate posts

Barn

Dutch Barn

House

Not to scale

more. Then the hedges close in again. The path can become rather overgrown at this point but this only lasts for a short distance beyond which it widens into a track lined with trees.

Follow the track past a wood on the right to where it emerges into an open space with a Dutch barn on the left. Walk past the barn and turn left on to a track coming from beside the wood on the right. This track leads back to the road.

Turn left and follow the verge for a short distance then cross the road to reach the car park.

49

Walk 13

Titchfield

$5\frac{1}{2}$ **miles (8.5 km)**

OS sheet 196
Start: Titchfield car park

Titchfield is a pleasant small town with a very interesting history. It lies in the Meon valley south of the main road to Portsmouth and forms a delightfully quiet backwater in what is otherwise a heavily industrialised area. Much of the land around the town is used for market-gardening and here are to be seen wide fields full of vegetables of every description.

Titchfield church is very old. Parts of it date back to Anglo-Saxon times and its fine Norman doorway is one of the best of its kind in the country. It is possible that it was at Titchfield that Shakespeare got his names for the characters old and young Gobbo, who appear in *The Merchant of Venice*. Shakespeare often stayed in the area with his friend and patron the Earl of Southampton and a William Gobbo was married here just three years before the play was written.

Another famous visitor to the area was Charles I. He stayed here with his queen during the first year of his reign and it was near here that he surrendered to Colonel Hammond in 1647.

The little river Meon, which gained its name from a Jutish tribe called Meonware who settled in the area during the fifth century, runs past the east end of the church on its way to join the Southampton Water. The valley through which it flows is very pleasant and near the estuary is a small nature reserve.

From the cliffs to the north of where the river Meon joins the sea there are magnificent views of the Isle of Wight and the Southampton Water. On the far shore Fawley Refinery is to be seen and to the north the docks at Southampton are visible on the horizon.

Leave the M27 at junction 9 and follow the A27 towards Farnham West and Titchfield. Take the third turning on the right. This is Southampton Hill and is signposted 'Titchfield village only'. The car park is to the right just beyond the fire station.

Leave the car park by following the signs to the High Street, a route that will lead you past a doctor's surgery on the right. At the road turn right and then left at the far end of The Square into Church Street. Bear right at the church on to a footpath skirting the churchyard. Ignore a path crossing it at right angles and carry straight on to the bridge over the river.

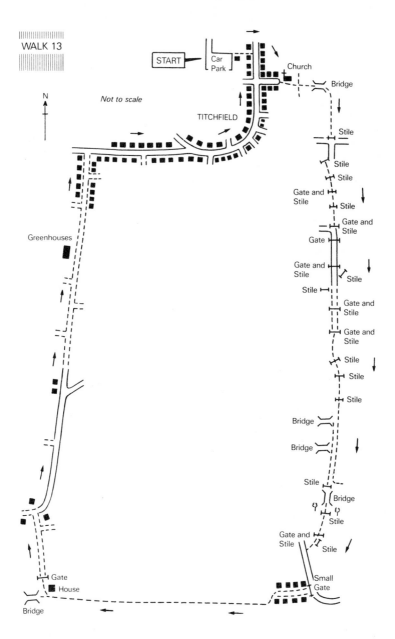

WALK 13

START
Car Park

N

Not to scale

TITCHFIELD

Church

Bridge

Stile
Stile
Stile
Gate and Stile
Stile
Gate and Stile
Gate
Gate and Stile
Stile
Stile
Gate and Stile
Gate and Stile
Stile
Stile
Stile
Bridge
Bridge
Stile
Bridge
Stile
Gate and Stile
Stile
Small Gate

Greenhouses

Gate
House
Bridge

At the far side of the bridge turn right and follow the river bank to a stile giving access to the road. Cross over and take the metalled track straight ahead.

At the far end is another stile. Cross this and follow the path through the meadow keeping the river on your right. The path will lead you across three more stiles, the second of which has a gate beside it, and on to another gate and stile. Beyond this there is a metalled track. Follow it straight ahead passing through the gap beside a second gate and then on through a third gate. Just the other side of this a stile leads into a field on the left but ignore it and carry on following the track which is now unmetalled. Cross three more stiles, the second and third being accompanied by gates, and where the track ends continue along the river bank. This will take you across three more stiles beyond the third of which a footpath leads to Titchfield Haven Local Nature Reserve.

Ignore two bridges to the right and follow the path, which widens into a track, until you come to a stile straight ahead. Disregard a path to the left at this point and go over the stile and the bridge beyond. The nature reserve is the area of marshland to your left. Follow the path through the trees and over another stile then go straight ahead towards some houses. Cross another stile beside a gate and follow the path to the road ignoring a stile to the left.

Turn left to follow the road to where it swings left by some beach huts and then turn right through a small gate marked 'Footpath only, no horses'. Walk along the gravel track straight ahead and turn left beyond the last beach hut on the left to pass through a gap between the hut and the fence. From here there are good views of the Solent and the Isle of Wight.

Turn right on to a narrow path leading along the cliff top and follow it for about a mile to where it dips down to the beach passing a house on the right. Just beyond the house turn right on to a path running up beside the garden.

The path leads to a gate which opens on to a track. Pass through the gap beside the gate and follow the track to the farm. Ignore a track to the right and continue for a short distance to where the track meets another in a T-junction. Turn right, passing the farmhouse on your left, and keep to the concrete track ignoring a gravel one leading to the left some distance beyond the farm. Where the track forks keep to the left-hand branch which goes straight ahead passing some houses on the left.

Just after the houses the track becomes unmetalled. Ignore a track to the left, another to the right and a third to the left and carry straight on passing the greenhouses on your left. This will bring you to where the track widens into an unmetalled lane. Go straight ahead ignoring any side turnings until you reach the road.

Turn right and follow the road to where it meets another from the left. Take the road called Coach Hill on the right and follow it down into the valley ignoring three turns to the right and one to the left.

Where the road ends in a T-junction turn left into South Street. Carry on across West Street and through The Square to the High Street then turn left beside The Queen's Head on to the path leading back to the car park.

Walk 14   Shawford and St Catherine's Hill

6 miles (9.5 km)

OS sheet 185
Start: Shawford village

Shawford is situated on the beautiful river Itchen which flows past Winchester on its way to join the Southampton Water. The part of the river north of Shawford is one of the most delightful in its entire length. Here it meanders through lush meadows and along its course a great variety of water fowl are to be seen.

St Catherine's Hill, which lies to the south-east of Winchester, is crowned by an early Iron Age hill-fort that dates from about 600 BC. From the summit there are good views of Winchester and its famous cathedral.

Prior to the Norman Conquest Winchester was, for a time, the capital of England. Amongst the kings who ruled from here were Alfred the Great and Canute. Its cathedral, the longest in England, was begun in the latter half of the eleventh century on a site adjoining that of the old seventh century minster which has since disappeared. Perhaps the site was not a good choice for the ground was very boggy and the cathedral had to be built on an enormous raft of timber. This was fairly successful but by the beginning of the twentieth century it had begun to sink; the buttresses were leaning and great cracks had appeared in the walls. The cathedral was saved from disaster by a diver named William Walker who spent five years working in the mud beneath the building, removing the peat handful by handful and replacing it with bags of concrete and concrete blocks.

One of the most interesting features on St Catherine's Hill is the ancient mizmaze. This is one of the few of its kind to be found in England. Nobody knows its original purpose but it is believed to have been used for religious rites in the pre-Christian era.

Turn off the Winchester by-pass on to the road to Shawford. As the road swings left just after entering the village turn right by the signpost marked 'To the Malms Restaurant'. There is a public car park on the right.

Walk back to the road and turn right to go under the railway bridge and pass some shops on the right. Ignore a footpath on the right beside the river bridge and turn left to cross the road and take a footpath on the far side of the bridge. This follows the river bank and then swings right across a narrow bridge where the waters divide. At the far side

54

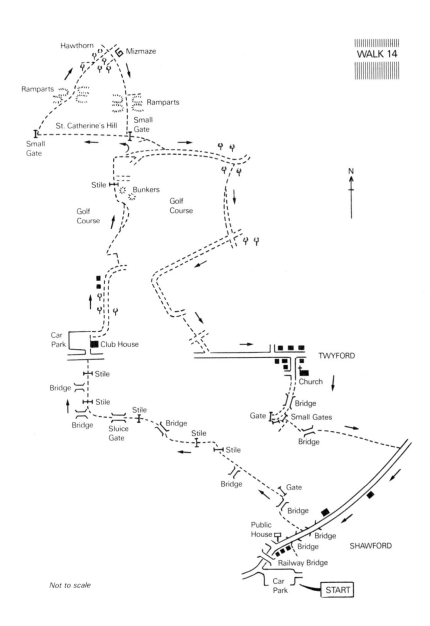

Hawthorn

Mizmaze

WALK 14

Ramparts

Ramparts

St. Catherine's Hill

Small Gate

Small Gate

N

Stile

Bunkers

Golf Course

Golf Course

Car Park

Club House

Stile

Bridge

Stile

Bridge

Bridge

Sluice Gate

Stile

Bridge

Stile

Bridge

TWYFORD

Church

Bridge

Gate

Small Gates

Bridge

Gate

Bridge

SHAWFORD

Public House

Bridge

Bridge

Railway Bridge

Not to scale

Car Park

START

turn left, ignoring a farm entrance on the right, and continue along the river bank.

Disregard another narrow bridge across the river and continue along the bank to cross a stile, then swing left to follow the river once more. This will bring you to a second stile. Cross it and continue to follow the river, going over another small bridge and a third stile.

Not far beyond this the path leads over a sluice gate where the river divides again and then goes straight on to swing right where two other branches of the river join. Ignore a narrow plank bridge which leads straight ahead at this point and follow the path round to the right, crossing two more stiles and passing another bridge on the left, to reach the road.

Cross over and take the footpath which leads through Hockley Golf Club car park. Keep the club house on your right and at the end of the car park swing right on to a track. This skirts the golf course on the left and then climbs a slope through a wood.

At the top the track leaves the trees, leads past some corrugated iron buildings on the left and becomes grass-covered. Where it swings right at the end of the field on the right leave it and go straight ahead for a very short distance before swinging sharp left to follow the edge of the green to a footpath sign. Turn right beside it and walk along the ridge with the valley on your left.

After some distance the narrow path becomes a track leading down into the valley. Cross the fairway keeping the bunkers on your right and climb the slope on the far side. Carry straight on passing the 15th tee on your left to reach a stile in the corner of the fence. Beyond this a track leads away to the right. Ignore it and carry straight on following the edge of the field with the fence on your left. There is a good view of St Catherine's Hill straight ahead.

At the far side of the field the grassy path becomes more visible. It swings right, giving a view of Winchester Cathedral in the valley to the left, and broadens into a track that leads down a slope.

At the bottom it is joined by a path from the left. Turn on to this and where the path forks take the right-hand branch going straight ahead. This will bring you to a small gate. Pass through it and continue along the valley until you come to another small gate. Turn right beside this and follow the narrow path leading up to the ramparts on the top of St Catherine's Hill, then go straight ahead towards the trees on the crest.

Follow the path straight through the trees on the far side of which is another good view of Winchester Cathedral. Walk past a small hawthorn bush on your left and then turn right. This will lead you past the mizmaze on your left. It is not very distinct but the patterning can still be discerned.

Ignore a path leading back into the trees at this point and carry straight on to reach the ramparts. Cross them and follow the path down the hillside. It is rather steep but quite an easy descent. Turn left through the small gate at the bottom and follow the path back to where it joins the track. Turn left and walk along it until you come to a place where it swings left. Turn sharp right at this point to take a path through the bushes ignoring a footpath sign straight ahead.

The path emerges from the bushes and climbs a slope to run between fences to the edge of the golf course. Continue to go straight ahead keeping the fence on your left. The track becomes more distinct and leads down into a valley on the far side of which it is crossed by another track. Turn right on to this keeping the golf course on your right. Eventually the track turns away from the golf course to run between fields. Continue along it for about another 150 yards to where it swings sharply left and then leave it to take a path veering slightly to the right between two hedges.

The path descends a slope to a track. Cross this and take the track straight ahead which leads down to the road. Turn left and walk up the hill to Twyford village. Go through the village until you come to Leeland House on the left then cross the road to take Church Lane leading straight ahead. Where the lane swings right carry straight on, passing the church on your left, to reach a gravel track. This will lead you across a bridge over the river. On the far side the track ends at a field gate but ignore this and go through the left of the two small gates straight ahead.

On the far side of this gate two paths diverge. Take the left-hand one which leads beside the hedge on the left and then turns left over a small bridge. Having crossed this small bridge, follow the fence on the left to the road. Cross over and turn right to walk back through Shawford village to the car park.

Walk 15 Calshot

3 miles (4.5 km)

OS sheet 196
Start: Stanswood Road, Calshot

Calshot lies south of Fawley on the western side of the entrance to the Southampton Water. It has a wide expanse of shingle beach and good views both of the Isle of Wight and the shipping lanes in which many interesting vessels are to be seen making their way to and from the Southampton docks.

The marshland which is protected by the spit of land that projects into the harbour mouth has been set aside as a conservation area by the County Council. The public are not allowed to enter the marshes but even from the path it is possible to enjoy the wide variety of bird life inhabiting them.

Take the A326 from Southampton to Fawley and, having passed Fawley Refinery on the left, follow the signs to Calshot. After $1\frac{1}{2}$ miles turn right opposite Fawley Power Station on to the road signposted 'Lepe $2\frac{3}{4}$'. This is Stanswood Road. Drive down it for just under 200 yards and then turn right on to a gravel track. Park on the right near where the track meets the road.

Start the walk by turning left to follow Stanswood Road back to the T-junction and then turn right. This will lead you past Fawley Power Station and Newtown Oyster Company on the left. Continue along the road until you come to a garage on the right and then turn left to cross a stile beside a field gate. Walk straight ahead skirting the fence on the right. This will eventually bring you to a stile with a small bridge beyond it. Cross both of these and follow the path which swings first to the left and then to the right passing Fawley Power Station on the left. This will bring you to where the path meets another in a T-junction at the edge of the marsh. This is the conservation area and beyond it are good views of the Southampton Water.

Turn right and follow the path. This runs between a fence on the right and the marsh on the left. Where the path divides near the far end of the fence, keep to the left fork. Continue along this for about 100 yards and then turn right on to a narrow path which heads towards the corner of the fence, and passes a small stretch of water on the left.

At the corner of the fence bear diagonally left across the grass towards a narrow wooden bridge. Cross this and the road beyond to pass between the beach huts on to the shingle. From here there are good views of the Solent and the Isle of Wight.

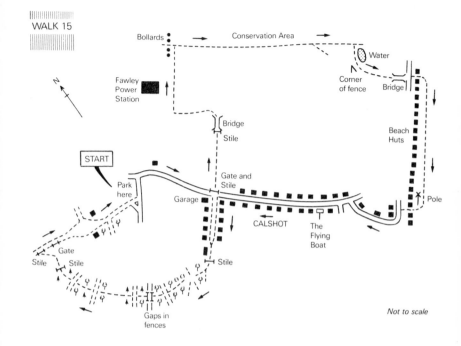

Turn right to follow the shingle with the beach huts on your right until you come to a yellow cross on a pole used as a guide for shipping. At this point leave the beach; turn right to pass back between the beach huts and then left to follow the road. This swings round to the right and is then joined by another road from the right. Carry straight on passing The Flying Boat on your left.

This will eventually bring you back to the garage which is also on your left. Turn left just before it on to an unmetalled track called Elmfield Lane. It goes past some houses and then degenerates into a path which leads to a stile.

Cross the stile and bear right to follow the path through the trees. It branches almost immediately but keep to the right-hand fork which leads to a clearing. Go straight ahead passing one path on the right and two on the left to take a fourth which skirts some holly bushes on the right.

When you come to where the path crosses a track carry straight on to reach a gap in the fence that gives access to a road. Cross this and go through a similar gap in the fence beside a gate on the opposite side and then follow the path straight ahead. It cuts between two stands of trees and is crossed by a track but ignore this and carry straight on.

The path crosses a valley and then enters some more trees where it

59

is crossed by a second track. Still go straight ahead and continue across a third track to reach a stile at the far side of the wood. Cross this and head straight across the field towards a gate on the far side. A little to the left of the gate is a stile. Cross this to reach the track and turn right. Ignore a track to the left where the main track widens and another to the right a little further on, then carry straight on to reach the place where you left the car.

Walk 16   Longparish

3 miles (4.5 km)

OS sheet 185
Start: Longparish village

As its name suggests Longparish village is very elongated. It stretches for almost a mile along the road which runs through the Test valley from Forton to Hurstbourne Priors. Parts of it are very pretty. There are several delightful thatched cottages and a lovely manor house backing on to the river.

The section of the river Test skirting Longparish has a beauty all of its own. It is very popular with fishermen for it is here that some of the biggest trout are to be caught. Just to the north of the village is an old water-mill. It has not been used for many years but parts of the water-wheel can still be seen through the holes in the boards that cover the lower windows.

Turn off the A303 3 miles east of Andover on to the road signposted 'Longparish 1 – B3048'. Follow this for 1½ miles and then turn left just opposite the Cricketers' Inn into a small housing estate. Follow the road round to the left where there is limited parking on the road.

Return to the main road and turn first left and then almost immediately right by the bus shelter to cross a stile in a fence set back from the road. Bear left to follow the footpath across the field passing the end of a fence on your left. This will bring you to another stile in the corner of the field. Cross it and go straight ahead across the footbridge over the river and the stile beyond. From here there are good views of Longparish House to the left.

Ignore a path leading through a small gate to the right and turn left to walk along a ridge of ground that runs across the field. This will bring you to a small plank bridge on the far side of which the path swings right to skirt the fence on the left.

In the corner of the field there is another stile with a plank bridge beyond it. Cross both of these and follow the river bank to the old mill. Turn left to pass the mill on your right and follow the lane to the road. Cross over and turn left to follow the road until you come to the gates of Longparish House on the left. Recross the road at this point and go over a stile just to the right of the gates to follow a narrow path across the field. This will give you another good view of Longparish House.

Leave the field by the stile at the far side and turn right to follow the road to the corner. Where it swings right go straight ahead follow-

WALK 16

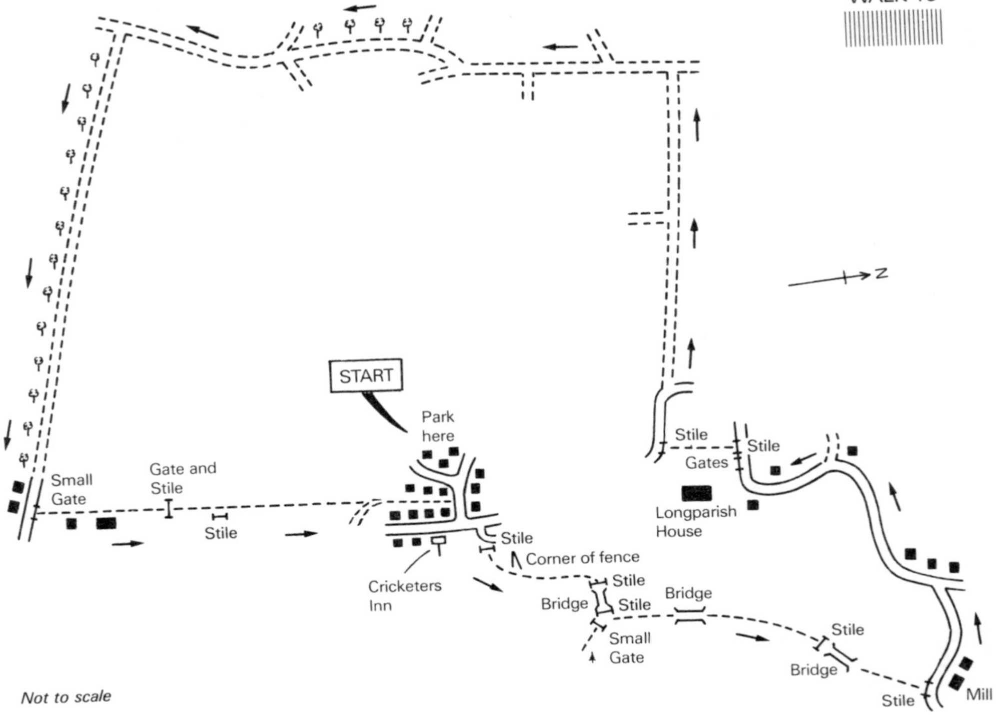

N

Not to scale

START

Park here

Stile

Gates

Longparish House

Stile

Stile

Stile

Mill

Stile

Bridge

Stile

Bridge

Bridge

Stile

Small Gate

Corner of fence

Stile

Cricketers Inn

Stile

Gate and Stile

Small Gate

ing a track which leads up a slope. Ignore a track to the left at the top of the hill and carry straight on to where the track meets a wider one in a T-junction. Turn left and follow this ignoring a track to the right and another to the left. Where the track divides take the right-hand fork skirting a wood on the right. Ignore a track to the right where the trees begin and one to the right and another to the left where the wood ends.

Beyond this the track swings right and descends a slight slope at the bottom of which it is joined by another track to the left. Turn left on to this. It follows a line of trees on the right and eventually joins the head of a metalled lane. Continue along this for about 25 yards and then turn left through a small gate into a field.

Follow the fence on the right to where the garden ends and then head straight across the field to reach a gate on the far side with a stile beside it. Cross the stile and follow the path straight ahead.

Ignore a stile in the fence to the right and carry on to where the path meets a track. Follow this straight ahead. It quickly narrows into a path running along beside some back gardens on the left to reach the road. This is the road that leads into the housing estate. Turn left and then left again to reach the place where you left your car.

5 miles (8 km)

OS sheet 185
Start: Farley Mount Country Park

Farley Mount Country Park is situated on the high chalk hills to the west of Winchester. It is an area of great natural beauty and magnificent views. From some places it is possible to see right across Hampshire to the hills around Salisbury and in others Southampton is visible on the horizon.

Farley Church is an interesting little early Norman church, standing in the fields at some distance from the nearest village. In its vestry is a beacon which dates back to the reign of Edward III and was used on Beacon Hill to alert those living in the area when danger threatened. The church also contains several memorials to members of the St John family. This family once owned the land around Farley but their home, which stood close to the church, has long since vanished.

The monument on Beacon Hill, the highest part of Farley Mount, was erected during the eighteenth century by Sir Paulet St John to the memory of a horse that saved his life. Whilst out hunting one day he came upon a chalk pit so suddenly that he had no time to stop. The horse leapt into the pit, a depth of over 20 feet, and landed without injury either to itself or its rider.

Take the A3090 from Hursley travelling towards Winchester and just over 1 mile beyond the village, turn left on to a lane signposted 'Farley Mount $2\frac{3}{4}$ – Sparsholt 3'. Take the first lane on the left, marked 'Farley Mount $2\frac{1}{2}$', and follow it to where it swings left to run along the ridge of Farley Mount. Turn right here on to the road to Winchester and then immediately left into the car park.

Return to the road and turn right to reach the junction. Cross over and go straight ahead through a wooden gate that opens on to a track. After a while the track becomes rather overgrown and runs between hedges to emerge at the edge of a field. From a gate on the right is a good view of the monument on Beacon Hill. Pass this gate and carry straight on to follow the path through some more bushes.

When the path leaves the bushes go straight ahead keeping the hedge on your right to reach a gate in the right-hand corner of the field. Cross the three-bar fence beside it and bear first left and then right on to a track. Disregard a stile on the edge of the wood to the right and follow the track. It is almost immediately joined by

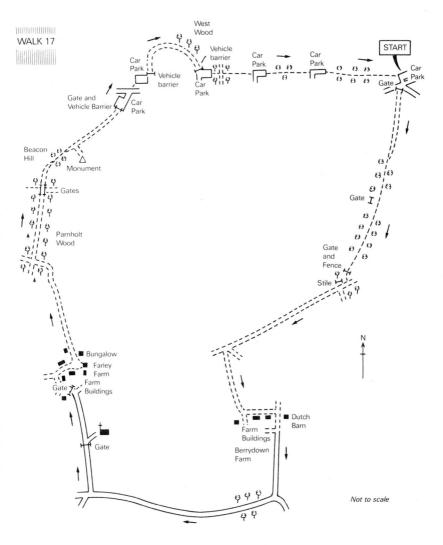

another track from the left. Ignore it and carry straight on. This will bring you to where the track is joined by two others from the left. Turn left on to the second of these which leads between two field fences.

At the farm turn left passing the farmhouse and some farm buildings on your right to reach the place where the track meets another in a T-junction. Turn right on to this passing the Dutch barn on your left. The track becomes a metalled drive and leads up to the road. At the junction turn right to follow the road up the hill, then carry on to the crossroads.

Turn right here on to the no through road to Farley Church. After some distance this goes through a gateway and forks. The right-hand branch leads to the church but keep to the left-hand branch which goes to the farm. Here it forks again. Take the left-hand branch through a gateway and then bear right to pass some farm buildings on your right.

Ignore two tracks to the left and bear right again and almost immediately left to pass a bungalow on your right. This will bring you on to a track which eventually leads to Parnholt Wood. As the track enters the edge of the wood it is crossed by another. Turn right on to this and follow it through the trees disregarding a grassy track which crosses it at right-angles and leading through gates on either side.

Eventually the track emerges from the wood and swings right to follow the curve of the hillside. From this point there are magnificent views to the left but these are soon blotted out as the track narrows into a path that leads through some bushes. On the far side of the bushes it widens again and a track to the right leads up to the Beacon Hill monument. This makes a worth-while diversion, not only to see the monument but also to enjoy the beautiful views.

After visiting the monument return to the track and follow it on down the slope and through the car park to the road. Cross over and bear slightly right into another car park. Turn right to cross this and then left to pass round a vehicle barrier on to a track. The track gradually swings round to the right and then goes through another vehicle barrier to meet the road.

Just beyond the vehicle barrier is a car park on the left. Turn into this and walk straight across it to reach a path which leads through the trees passing a litter bin on your right. It is crossed almost immediately by a track but ignore this and carry straight on to where the path leaves the trees. Here it ends. Go straight ahead across the edge of the grassy slope keeping the road on your right.

This will bring you to another car park. Walk straight across it and take a path on the far side that leads through the bushes to yet another car park. Cross this and follow the path to where it emerges from the bushes. The car park where you left the car is straight ahead.

Walk 18   Denny Lodge

3 miles (4.5 km)

OS sheet 196
Start: Blackdown car park

The area of wood and heathland to the south-east of Lyndhurst is one of the most beautiful parts of the New Forest. There are magnificent views to be seen here as well as several features of interest.

Beside the railway line to the north of Beaulieu Road Station are the wooden pens where the Beaulieu Road Pony Sales are held. Originally the sales were held at Lyndhurst Fair on Swan Green but as traffic in the town increased this became impractical and so they were moved to their present site. The sales are held here in April, August, September, October and November.

To the south of the Beaulieu Road lies the Bishop of Winchester's Purlieu, a stretch of bog approximately 1 mile in length and $\frac{1}{2}$ mile wide surrounded by a medieval earthwork known as Bishop's Dyke. The area which the earthwork encloses is said to have been a piece of church land granted to the Bishop of Winchester by the King.

According to an old story the King promised to give the Bishop as much land in the forest as he could crawl round on his hands and knees in a day. It is possible that by this method he had not thought to lose much but the Bishop was an active man and managed to crawl right round an area which provided some of the best opportunities for hunting snipe to be found in the forest. This is a good story but not necessarily a true one. The very fact that the shape of the Bishop's Dyke is so irregular tends to belie it. It is possible that the dyke was merely built to enclose a fish pond.

Take the B3056 from Lyndhurst travelling towards Beaulieu. Blackdown car park is about 3 miles along this road on the left.

Return to the road and turn left to follow the verge for about 25 yards before turning left again on to a track. Walk along this until you come to where it meets another track in a T-junction and go straight ahead to cross the bridge over the railway. At the far side of the bridge six tracks diverge. Take the one skirting the railway fence on the right and follow it to the pens where the pony sales are held. Here the track is joined by another from the left and leads on to the road passing the pens on the right.

At the road cross over and turn right to go across the bridge. It is advisable to be very careful for there is no pavement. However, the bridge is regularly used by passengers who go through the small gates

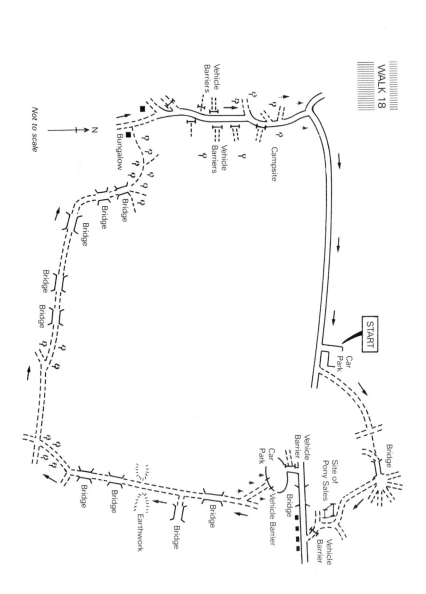

WALK 18

Not to scale

N

Vehicle
Barriers

Vehicle
Barriers

Campsite

Bungalow

Bridge

Bridge

Bridge

Bridge

Bridge

START

Car
Park

Bridge

Vehicle
Barrier

Vehicle
Barrier

Car
Park

Site of
Pony Sales

Vehicle
Barrier

Vehicle Barrier

Bridge

Bridge

Bridge

Earthwork

Bridge

Bridge

on the top of it to reach the station platforms so the majority of motorists are on the look-out for pedestrians.

Having crossed the bridge turn left into Shatterford car park. Leave this by the track which goes through a vehicle barrier in the rear left-hand corner and where this merges with another just beyond a clump of fir trees carry straight on.

The track crosses a plank bridge, climbs a slight slope and then divides. The left-hand fork crosses another bridge over the railway so take the right one going straight ahead. About 100 yards along it the embankment bordering the purlieu crosses the track at right-angles.

The track goes over two more plank bridges and then comes to a group of trees where it divides. Take the right-hand fork which passes a large oak tree on the right and then emerges from the first belt of trees to be crossed by a second track. Turn right on to this and where it divides keep to the right-hand fork which is the more distinct.

This leads into the trees and then comes out of them again to cross three plank bridges. Beyond the third it becomes very indistinct. Go straight on for a very short distance and then swing right towards the wood. This will take you across two more bridges on the far side of which two paths lead into the trees. Take the left-hand one going straight ahead and where it forks take the left-hand branch. This skirts the fence on the left to reach a track.

Turn right and follow the track up the slope. At the top it becomes metalled and is joined by another track from the left. Ignore this and go straight on disregarding another gravel track which leads through a vehicle barrier to the left. Beyond this the metalled track goes through a campsite. Keep to it ignoring all side turnings until you come to the place where it joins the road. Turn right and follow the verge back to the car park, on the left.

Walk 19   Longstock

6 miles (9.5 km)

OS sheet 185
Start: Longstock church

The pretty little village of Longstock lies in the Test valley to the
north of Stockbridge. It contains several delightful thatched cottages
and near Longstock House, to the north of the village, are some water
gardens that are often open to the public during the summer months.

In the Dark Ages the area around Longstock was the haunt of
Danish invaders who made their way up the river Test in their small
ships. They had a dock at Longstock where they would stop to refur-
bish and repair their craft before putting to sea once more. It was near
here, at Andover, that King Ethelred made the first payment of
'Danegeld' to Olaf the Dane.

To the west of Longstock is Danebury Hill. In spite of its name this
is an Iron Age hill-fort. It is the finest of its kind in Hampshire covering
13 acres and being defended by a triple line of ramparts and ditches.

On the high ground to the east of Longstock there is a radio
telescope and good views of this may be obtained on several parts of
the walk.

Take the A3057 from Stockbridge travelling towards Andover and
after ½ mile turn left on to a lane signposted 'Longstock ½'. The lane
crosses the river and ends in a T-junction in Longstock village. Turn
left and then right by the church. Park on the left just opposite the
cemetery.

Walk back past the church and turn left to take the road running
through the village. Ignore the turning to the right by The Peat Spade
Inn and carry straight on to where the road turns sharp left by
Corner Cottage. Leave it at this point and take a track leading straight
ahead.

The track is fairly short and ends at a gate. Go through this and
follow the hedge on the right to a stile in the far corner of the field.
Cross the stile and continue to follow the hedge. This will bring you
to a fence. Cross it and go on along the hedge for a short distance
until you come to a small gate on the right. Pass through this and
turn sharp left to reach a gate with a small gate beside it in the corner
of the field. Go through the small gate and take the track straight
ahead to the road.

Turn right to follow the verge. This will lead you past the grounds
of Longstock House on the left and gives views of the radio telescope

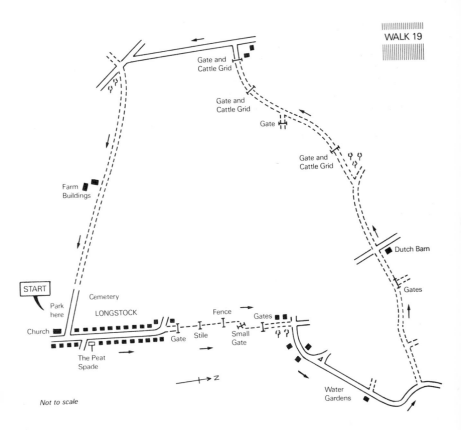

straight ahead. After about ½ mile Longstock Water Gardens are on the right.

Having passed a cottage called North Lodge on the right, continue along the road for about ¼ mile and then turn left on to a track at a point where the road curves right. The track runs through a valley. Ignore a track leading up a slope to the right and go straight on. This will take you past another track that goes through a pair of gates to the right marked 'Private' and will eventually bring you to where the track joins a road.

Cross over and take the wide track straight ahead. Where this divides keep to the left-hand fork which skirts a wood on the right and then crosses a cattle grid with a gate beside it. Beyond this the track borders a field on the right. It is joined by another track from the left but this is marked 'Private Road' so ignore it and carry straight on. The track crosses two more cattle grids with gates beside them and then passes some farm buildings on the right to reach the road.

Turn left to follow the road up to the T-junction. From here are

71

good views of Danebury Hill, slightly to the right and crowned with a grove of beech trees.

At the road junction turn left and then sharp left again on to a track which passes some trees on the right. The track leads over the brow of a hill, from which there is another good view of the radio telescope and then passes some farm buildings on the right. Beyond this point the track widens into an unmetalled lane. It leads down a slope and then becomes metalled. The place where you parked the car is further down it on the right.

8 miles (12.5 km)

OS sheet 196
Start: Balmer Lawn car park

This walk is in one of the most interesting areas of the New Forest. Parts of it are open heathland and parts dense woodland where walkers may be lucky enough to catch a glimpse of the timid Japanese sika deer. These creatures, once regarded as sacred animals in their native country, have white rumps and white-spotted coats. They were originally kept in captivity by Lord Montagu on his estate at Beaulieu but, in 1904, a pair escaped. The following year he released another pair to join them and now there are about sixty living wild in the woods around Brockenhurst.

William Gilpin, the famous author and naturalist, was once the minister of Boldre church. His book *Scenery of the New Forest* was one of the most popular works on natural history to be written during the eighteenth century. Gilpin is buried in Boldre churchyard where his grave is to be seen to the north of the church.

Brockenhurst church is the only forest church mentioned in the Domesday Book. In its churchyard are a group of graves dating back to World War I and the grave of another famous New Forest personality, Brusher Mills.

Brusher Mills, who gained his nickname from the careful way in which he swept the Balmer Lawn cricket pitch between innings, made his living by catching snakes. These he sold to London Zoo where they were used to feed the king cobras. He was very quick and deft in his work and could pick up an adder in his bare hands without getting bitten.

Balmer Lawn is one of the open grassy areas which are such a feature of the New Forest. It once served as a race course where New Forest pony races were held. On its border is the Balmer Lawn Hotel. This was the operational headquarters used by General Eisenhower and General Montgomery prior to the invasion of France in World War II.

Take the A337 from Lyndhurst to Brockenhurst and on the outskirts of the town turn left just beyond the Balmer Lawn Hotel on to the road signposted 'Beaulieu 6 – B3055'. Park in Balmer Lawn car park on the right just beyond the turning.

Leave the car park and walk on down the B3055 passing Balmer Lawn Hotel on your left. Where the buildings on the left end and the

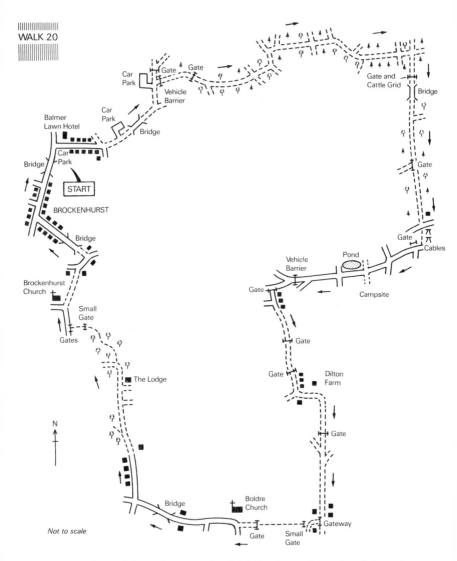

road swings right take a track which leads straight ahead ignoring another to the left signposted 'Private Properties Only'. The track runs past Tilery Road car park on the left and over a bridge some distance beyond which it divides. Take the left fork marked 'Car park 150 yards'.

Turn right beside Standing Hat car park on to a track leading through a vehicle barrier and ignore another track going through a gate straight ahead. The track swings right through a gate and is joined by another track from the right. Ignore this and carry straight on, then keep to the gravel track ignoring all side turnings.

Where the track is crossed by another gravel one still go straight ahead disregarding all side turnings until the track passes a plantation of mature fir trees on the right and is crossed by a second gravel track. Turn right here and follow the track through the gate and over the bridge which crosses the railway line. Ignore one track to the left and another to the right and keep to the main track until you come to the road.

Cross over and follow the line of overhead electricity cables to a metalled track bordering a campsite, then turn right. Ignore a gate to the right and a track to the left. This will bring you to where the track meets another in a T-junction. Turn left and then almost immediately right to pass a chemical closet emptying point on your left.

Where the track is crossed by an unmetalled one go straight on passing the pond on your right. This will bring you to a point where the track is crossed by a second coming from the entrance to the campsite. Go straight over this and on along the track marked 'Overflow campsite'.

Ignore a track to the left and follow the one you are on through the vehicle barrier. Beyond this it divides. Take the left-hand fork and then turn left through a gate signposted 'Bridleway'. Within a very short distance the track divides. Keep to the left. After this it leads down into a valley, goes through a gate and then climbs a slope to a farm.

Go through the gate beside the farm building and follow the track round to the left passing a cowshed and a Dutch barn on the left. The track swings right to skirt a field on the right and then goes through a gate. Here it is joined by another track from the right. Ignore this track and another on the left and carry straight on. The track widens into an unmetalled lane. It passes a pair of houses and some farm buildings on the left and a wooden machinery shed on the right with a thatched farmhouse beside it.

Turn right to go through a gateway between the shed and the farmhouse. As the track turns left to enter the grounds of the house, go through a small wooden gate straight ahead and follow the path keeping the fence on your left. At the far end of the field another, larger gate opens on to a track which leads straight ahead passing Boldre churchyard on the right. This is the churchyard where William Gilpin is buried and it is worth pausing here to find his grave.

Where the track joins the lane turn right. The lane goes steadily down hill, is joined by another lane from the left and crosses the Lymington River before climbing a slight slope to a crossroads. Turn right here on to the no through road to Blazemore Farm. Beyond the farm the lane becomes a track. Follow it for about $\frac{1}{2}$ mile to where, having passed a cottage called The Lodge on the right, it climbs a slope and swings left. At this point it is joined by a path going straight ahead.

Take the path which skirts some fields on the right and then winds its way through woodland before cutting between some more fields to meet the road. Go through the small gate and turn right to follow the road to Brockenhurst church where Brusher Mills is buried. To find his grave take the path behind the church leading down into the churchyard. The war graves are on the right and Brusher Mills' grave is between them and the path.

The walk continues along the track which runs down a slope passing the churchyard on the left. Where this track joins a road turn right and then almost immediately left on to another track leading to a footbridge over the railway. Cross the bridge and follow the lane straight ahead to reach the road. Turn right to follow the road out of Brockenhurst. The car park is on the right just beyond the bridge over the river.

Walk 21   Rhinefield Ornamental Drive

$2\frac{1}{2}$ miles (4 km)

OS sheet 195
Start: Brock Hill car park

This is one of the most attractive and interesting of the New Forest walks. It includes a large number of features of interest to the naturalist and the easy walking conditions make it an ideal choice for a family outing. The walk is particularly lovely in early summer when the trees are in full leaf and the rhododendrons, which line parts of the ornamental drive, are in flower.

The Rhinefield Ornamental Drive gets its name from Rhinefield Lodge which was originally the home of the Master Keeper. Before the present road was built in 1938 the lodge was approached by a gravel drive. In 1859 an avenue of young conifers was planted along the length of this drive. It consisted of a wide variety of species including redwoods, Douglas fir, Austrian pine and deodar cedar. In the century since they were planted many of these trees have grown to be the tallest of their kind in the British Isles.

The first part of the walk takes in a section of the Forestry Commission's Brock Hill forest walk. As its name suggests, this runs through an area of the forest frequented by badgers and, although these shy nocturnal creatures are rarely to be seen, a number of their setts are visible beneath the trees.

Vinney Ridge Inclosure is one of the oldest inclosures in the New Forest. It was first set aside for growing oak and beech in 1700. In those days large numbers of these hardwood trees were needed to build the wooden sailing ships on which Britain depended for her trade and defence. The young trees were protected by a ditch bordering a 6 feet high bank with a wooden fence on top to keep out deer, cattle and ponies.

Black Water is one of many streams draining this part of the forest. It is a tributary of the Lymington River and gains its name from the dark colour of its water. This becomes discoloured as it passes through the peat bogs further north.

Take the A35 from Lyndhurst travelling towards Bournemouth. After 2 miles turn left at the crossroads on to the narrow road signposted 'Rhinefield'. Within a very short distance the road becomes lined with laurel and rhododendron bushes. Pass a gravel track which crosses the road at right-angles and turn right just beyond it into Brock Hill car park.

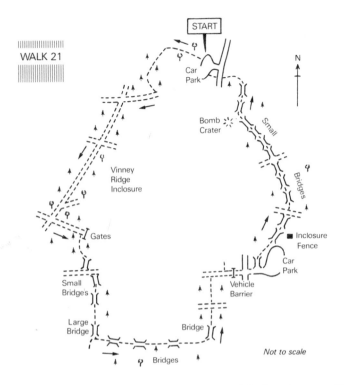

WALK 21

START

Car
Park

Bomb
Crater

Small

N

Bridges

Vinney
Ridge
Inclosure

Gates

Inclosure
Fence

Car
Park

Vehicle
Barrier

Small
Bridges

Large
Bridge

Bridge

Bridges

Not to scale

Leave the car park by the path in the rear right-hand corner. This is labelled 'Brock Hill Walk'. It leads up a slope through a grove of oak and beech trees and near the top some old badger setts are to be seen amongst the trees on the right. Beyond them the path swings left into a stand of young conifers. Continue along the path until it turns left again and is joined by a grassy track from the right. Turn right on to this and follow it for a short distance to where it is crossed by a gravel track, then turn left.

Within about 200 yards this track is crossed by another. Disregard it and carry straight on. You will soon emerge from the plantation of mature conifers into an area where young fir trees are interspersed with older hardwoods. The track leads on through these trees until, having been joined by a grassy track from the left, it is crossed by another gravel one.

Turn left on to this track and follow it until you reach the place where it is barred by a pair of gates. Do not go through these gates but turn right beside them on to a gravel path which skirts the fence on the left for a very short distance before winding away through the trees.

The path crosses a plank bridge, turns left to follow the course of a grassy track for a short distance and then swings right again to cross two more small bridges. It then leads on through the trees to a larger wooden bridge which spans the Black Water. On the far side of this bridge turn sharp left, disregarding a rather muddy path leading straight ahead, to follow the gravel path running along the bank. It crosses three small plank bridges and then, as it approaches the road, swings left once more to recross the Black Water by a second, larger bridge.

Go over the bridge and continue along the path which cuts across a rather boggy grassy track and then meets a gravel one that leads up to a gate on the left. Turn right on to this track and follow it down past the vehicle barrier to the road. Cross over and turn left across the small plank bridge passing the Forestry Commission sign on your right. Skirt the edge of the car park to reach the beginning of 'Tall Trees Walk' then follow the narrow gravel path straight ahead.

Within a short distance this will lead you past a reconstruction of the old inclosure fence on the right, just one of several interesting features which border the path and are marked by Forestry Commission signs. Another, which lies to the left of the path about $\frac{1}{4}$ mile further on, is a bomb crater made during World War II at a time when the Germans were dropping a number of incendiary and high-explosive bombs on the forest. Their intention was to burn down the trees that were providing Britain with an important source of timber.

Beyond the bomb crater the path, which by this time has crossed nine small plank bridges and two grassy tracks, swings to the right. It passes over another two plank bridges, between which it is crossed by a narrow path, and then turns left to join the road. Cross over and you will find Brock Hill car park to your right.

3 miles (4.5 km)

OS sheet 196
Start: Keyhaven car park

This is a pleasant coastal walk which provides beautiful views of the Solent and the Isle of Wight. Parts of it run along the edge of marshland where a variety of birdlife is to be seen and in other places there are good views of the small craft that frequent the Lymington River.

Hurst Castle stands at the end of a narrow spit of land stretching out from Keyhaven towards the Isle of Wight. The castle was built by Henry VIII as part of his coastal defences at a time when he was expecting a French invasion. Today little of the original building can be seen for it is almost completely enclosed by two extensions added during the reign of Queen Victoria.

For a short period in the seventeenth century Hurst Castle was used as a prison for Charles I. He was brought here from Carisbrooke Castle on the Isle of Wight in November 1648 but was soon moved to Windsor and from there to London for his trial.

Take the A337 from Christchurch travelling towards Lymington. After 4 miles turn on to the B3058 to Milford on Sea. Follow this road for $3\frac{1}{2}$ miles and then turn right again on to a road signposted 'Keyhaven 1'. Drive straight through the village, passing the war memorial on your left, and park in the car park opposite The Gun Inn.

Leave the car park passing the public conveniences on your right and turn right opposite The Gun Inn. Ignore a footpath to the right and follow the road over the bridge, then turn right to cross a stile on to a narrow path skirting the water. From here there are good views of Hurst Castle straight ahead.

The path follows the water's edge for some distance before swinging right and then left to lead along the top of a causeway that separates the sea from the saltmarshes. Cross another stile where the causeway turns right and continue to follow it round to the left. From here there are magnificent views of the Isle of Wight.

The path will bring you to a second stile beyond which a jetty runs out into the sea on the right. Cross this stile and pass the jetty to continue along the causeway ignoring a second stile giving access to a track on the left. After about $1\frac{1}{2}$ miles the causeway swings left to skirt a small inlet near the mouth of the Lymington River. As the inlet turns right the path divides. Take the right-hand fork, cross a stile and continue, keeping the water on your right. Where this ends there

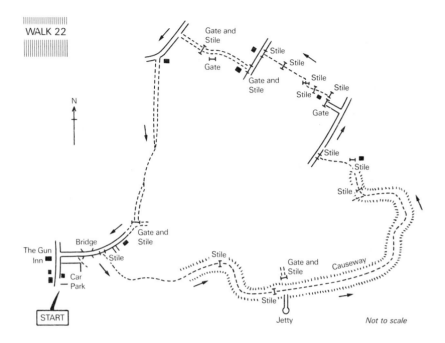

is another stile straight ahead but ignore it and turn left to follow the path to the road.

Turn right and walk along the road until you come to another road on the left. This is signposted 'Footpath' and is quite a short cul-de-sac. Follow it to the end and bear right to take a path leading over a stile. This will take you past a house on the left to a second stile. Go over it and follow the fence on the right for a short distance to reach a stile on the right. On the far side of this turn left to walk along the edge of the field with the fence on your left. Cross a stile in the corner of the field and go straight on to reach another which gives access to a lane.

Turn left to follow the lane for about 25 yards and then turn right through a gate with a stile beside it on to a track marked 'Public Footpath'. Continue along this track until you come to where it meets a metalled lane in a T-junction. Turn left and follow this for a very short distance to where it swings right and then take the track straight ahead passing a concrete block building on your left.

After some distance the track temporarily degenerates into a path, crosses the corner of a field and follows a hedge on the right before widening into a track once more. It then leads to a gate with a stile beside it. Go over this and take the track straight ahead ignoring one to the left. The track quickly becomes a metalled lane. This will lead you back over the bridge to the road junction at The Gun Inn where the car park is on the left.

81

Walk 23   Holidays Hill Inclosure

3 miles (4.5 km)

OS sheet 195
Start: Millyford Bridge car park

Holidays Hill Inclosure lies to the south-west of Lyndhurst and contains some of the most interesting features to be found in the New
Forest. Not far from the car park is a Portuguese fireplace. This is a
relic of World War I when Portuguese troops were stationed in the
area to help the depleted local labour force produce timber for the
war effort. The fireplace, once part of the cookhouse, is retained as a
memorial and was restored by the Forestry Commission who were
given financial assistance with the project by the Portuguese government.

The Knightwood Oak is one of the largest trees in the New Forest.
It is over three hundred years old and has been pollarded. This is an
old custom no longer practised in the forest. When a tree was pollarded
the top section of the trunk was removed so that the branches grew
fairly close to the ground and the foliage was within reach of the forest
animals.

Not far from the Knightwood Oak is Holidays Hill Cottage where
there is a collection of amphibians and reptiles. Nearly every species
of these creatures to be found in the British Isles is represented here.

Leave the A35 just west of Lyndhurst to take the road signposted
'Emery Down ¼'. Turn left at the New Forest Inn on to the road
marked 'Bolderwood 4 – Linwood 7' and follow it for just over a mile.
At this point Millyford Bridge car park is on the right.

Walk back to the road, cross over and turn right to follow the verge.
This will lead you past a barbecue site on the left and, just beyond,
the Portuguese fireplace.

Carry on along the verge for a short distance and then turn left
through a gate into the inclosure. Follow the gravel track straight
ahead ignoring a grassy one to the right and where the gravel track
divides take the right-hand fork. Walk along it for about 25 yards and
then turn right again on to another gravel track that almost immediately curves to the left. Keep to this track ignoring a grassy one to
the left, another to the right and a third which crosses it.

Just beyond this the track swings left again. Ignore a grassy track
to the right at this point and then another to the right and one to the
left as the main track swings left yet again.

The track descends a slight slope and near the bottom it is crossed

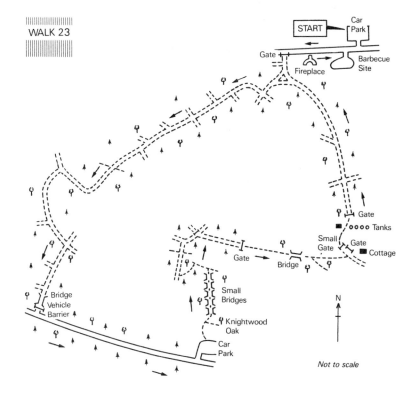

START

Car Park

Gate

Barbecue Site

Fireplace

Gate

Tanks

Small Gate

Gate

Cottage

Gate

Bridge

Small Bridges

Bridge
Vehicle Barrier

Knightwood Oak

Car Park

N

Not to scale

by a path. Disregard this and keep to the track as it curves to the right. Ignore a very rutted track to the right as the main track swings left again and yet another to the right further along. Not far beyond this the track is crossed by another. Turn right on to this and follow it through the trees ignoring all side turnings until it crosses a bridge and joins the road. Turn left and walk along the road until you come to Knightwood Oak car park on the left.

Go into the car park and turn left on to a narrow path signposted 'To Knightwood Oak'. This path has been laid out by the Forestry Commission for the use of visitors and along its route are some interesting items to show how pollarding was done.

At the Knightwood Oak the path divides. Take the left-hand branch which passes the tree on the right and follow it to where it turns right beside the inclosure fence. Leave it at this point and turn left along the bank keeping the fence on your right. After about 100 yards the path turns left away from the fence. Follow it to where it joins a grassy track and turn right. Ignore a path crossing the track where the fence begins on the left and carry straight on.

This will bring you to where the track joins a gravel one. Follow the gravel one straight ahead for a very short distance and then turn right on to a grassy track. This leads to a gate. Go through it and follow the path straight ahead keeping the fence on your right. Where the fence ends, head straight across the clearing to cross a small plank bridge and then go up the slope towards a white building. This is Holidays Hill Cottage. Turn left just before it to go through a small gate between a Forestry Commission sign and another marked 'Car park'. Walk straight ahead to pass a hut on your left. The tanks containing the amphibians and reptiles are on your right.

Leave the cottage grounds by a track leading through a gate behind the tanks. Ignore a track which crosses it and another grassy one that leads to the left and keep to the main track until you come to where it forks. Take the right-hand branch leading to a gate opening on to the road. Turn right and follow the verge back to the car park on the left.

3 miles (4.5 km)

OS sheet 195
Start: Stoney Cross car park

Anyone who has had any contact with English history will be familiar with the story of William Rufus and the mystery which surrounds his death. William Rufus was the son of William the Conqueror and became king in 1087. Thirteen years later he was shot in the back by an arrow whilst out hunting in the New Forest and killed. Nobody really knows whether his death was an act of murder and, if so, who the culprit really was. The blame was cast upon one of his fellow huntsmen Walter Tyrrell, Lord of Poix, who was forced to flee for his life after the incident. Yet Tyrrell, an excellent marksman, proclaimed to his dying day that he had nothing to do with the King's death.

Rufus Stone, which stands in the New Forest just south-west of Cadnam, is said to mark the spot where William Rufus died. The original stone was erected in 1745 by Lord Delaware when he was Master Keeper at Bolderwood Lodge. It was later covered by an iron casing to protect it from vandals.

The area around Stoney Cross is high land from which there are magnificent views to the east. During World War II this part of the forest was used as an aerodrome and sections of the old runways are still to be seen here.

Kings Garn Gutter is one of the many streams that drain the forest area. It gained its strange name because it runs through what was once a garn or garden where the king's beehives were kept.

Turn off the A35 just west of Lyndhurst to take the road signposted 'Emery Down $\frac{1}{4}$ – Bolderwood'. Follow this for $\frac{1}{4}$ mile and turn left beside the New Forest Inn on to the road signposted 'Bolderwood 4 – Linwood 7'. Drive on for 5 miles and turn right on to the road marked 'Stoney Cross $2\frac{1}{2}$ – Fritham $3\frac{1}{2}$'. Where this ends in a T-junction turn right. Pass the entrance to Longbeech caravan camp on the left and, just beyond the expanse of concrete on the right, turn left into Stoney Cross car park.

Take the metalled track which runs at right-angles across the top of the car park and turn left to walk towards Stoney Cross keeping the road on the right. After a while there are good views to the left and then the track joins the road. Bear left at this point to follow the verge for about 75 yards to where a narrow path goes slightly left just before a track on the far side of the road. Take this path. It curves left

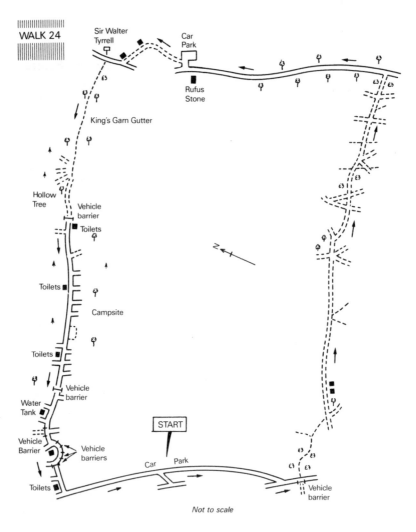

Sir Walter Tyrrell

Car Park

Rufus Stone

King's Garn Gutter

Hollow Tree

Vehicle barrier

Toilets

Toilets

Campsite

Toilets

Water Tank

Vehicle Barrier

Vehicle barriers

Vehicle barrier

START

Car Park

Vehicle barrier

Toilets

Not to scale

through the bushes and is joined by another path from the left. Ignore
this and go straight on to where the path meets a grassy track which
immediately divides.

Take the left-hand fork which will lead you past two houses on the
right and on along the ridge. Ignore two paths to the right and where
the track branches four ways take the second track from the left. This
goes straight ahead passing a clump of trees on the left. Within a few
yards the track branches again. Take the right-hand fork. This will
bring you to where the track is crossed by two tracks from the right

that converge on the left. Ignore them and carry straight on to follow the track through the bushes.

At the far side the track is crossed by a path at a point where four tracks join. Take the left of two tracks ahead of you. Ignore a path and a track which cross the track you are on, a path to the right and a second cross track and carry straight on until you reach the road. Turn left to follow the road down the hill to Rufus Stone which is on the left.

Cross the road to Rufus Stone car park and take the track marked 'Access to cottage'. Walk down to the cottage and turn left beside the garden gate to follow the hedge on the right. This leads you past another cottage to the road. Turn right to pass the Sir Walter Tyrrell public house on your right then cross the road near the far end of the car park. This will lead you past a 'Feeding of Animals Prohibited' sign on to the grass. Veer slightly right, passing between a clump of bushes on the left and a hedge on the right, to reach a point where the path becomes more distinct. It leads straight ahead and then dips down to a stream. This is Kings Garn Gutter.

There is no bridge but it is usually easy to cross unless there has been heavy rain. In this case follow the bank for a short distance to the left where the stream narrows and it is possible to step across.

Follow the path up the slope on the far side of the stream to where it emerges on to an expanse of grass. Curve slightly left to take a path at the far side passing a hollow dead tree on your right. From here the track becomes more distinct. Follow it up a slope and then go straight ahead taking a concrete track leading through a vehicle barrier into a campsite. Follow it straight through the campsite ignoring any side turnings.

The track climbs steadily up a gentle slope and eventually passes through another traffic barrier at the far end of the campsite. Go round the barrier and continue to follow the track straight ahead passing a water tank on your right.

Beyond the tank the track curves left to the campsite entrance. Pass this on your right following the sign 'Way Out'. Ignore two tracks through vehicle barriers on the left and turn left on to a third. Follow this to where it meets another in a T-junction and turn left. This is the far end of Stoney Cross car park. Go straight ahead to reach the place where you left your car.

Walk 25   Wilverley and the Naked Man

5 miles (8 km)

OS sheet 195
Start: Wilverley Inclosure car park

This walk provides a wide variety of scenery and interesting features. Parts of it cross open heathland, others lead through mature inclosures or skirt some of the wide expanses of grass known as lawns where the forest ponies and cattle graze. From Wilverley Plain there are magnificent views across the forest and near the beginning of the walk the tall column of Sway tower can be seen on the horizon to the south.

Sway tower, or Peterson's Folly, was built during the latter half of the nineteenth century by Judge Peterson in an effort to relieve local unemployment and to prove that concrete was a durable building material. When it was first erected the tower, which is 218 feet high, had a light at the top. However, this proved to be a great hazard to sailors in the Solent who mistook it for a lighthouse and the Admiralty demanded that the light be removed.

The track leading across Wilverley Plain to the Naked Man is a section of an ancient ridgeway and was once part of a well-used route between Burley and Lymington. During the eighteenth and early nineteenth centuries, when smuggling was rife in the forest area, it was often used by smugglers on their nocturnal excursions to bring contraband inland.

The Naked Man, which stands to the right of this track near the point where it joins the main road, is the remains of an oak tree that has been struck by lightning. It was once used as a gibbet.

Leave the main A35, Christchurch to Lyndhurst road, at Holmsley to follow signs to Brockenhurst and Setthorns. Where the road forks beyond the cattle grid take the left-hand branch, marked Brockenhurst and Lymington. This will lead you up a slope passing the entrance to a car park on the right. Not far beyond it a gravel track leads to a second car park at the edge of the inclosure on the left. This is Wilverley Inclosure car park.

Walk back along the gravel track to the road and turn right to follow the verge to the car park sign. Cross over and take the gravel track bearing right through Yew Tree Bottom car park. In the far left-hand corner of the car park a narrow path leads to a picnic place. Follow this for a short distance and then bear slightly left to walk down through the valley passing a wooden picnic table on your left.

This will bring you to an embankment which once supported a

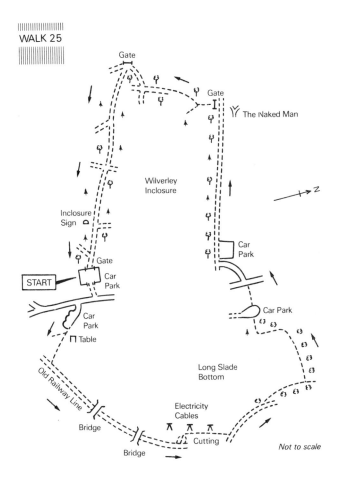

Gate

Gate

The Naked Man

Wilverley
Inclosure

Z

Inclosure
Sign

Gate

Car
Park

START

Car
Park

Car
Park

Car
Park

Table

Car
Park

Old Railway Line

Long Slade
Bottom

Electricity
Cables

Bridge

Cutting

Bridge

Not to scale

railway line to Brockenhurst. Climb the embankment and turn left to
follow the course of the old railway. Continue along the railway line
until you have passed under two bridges. Beyond the second the bank
on the left becomes lower and after about 75 yards a cutting gives
access to the lawn beyond. Go through the cutting and turn right to
follow the electricity cables to a gravel path that comes through a
broken railway bridge on the right.

Turn left and follow the path to where a short gravel path leads
through the gorse bushes on to the lawn on the left. Take this path
and then swing right up the slope keeping the gorse bushes on your
right. At the top right-hand corner of the lawn a path leads straight
ahead to rejoin the gravel one. Ignore this and turn left to follow the
edge of the lawn along the hillside. After about $\frac{1}{2}$ mile the perimeter

of the lawn curves left down the slope to the valley and then right, passing a lone fir tree on the left, to end at a car park. Cross the turning circle at the lower end of the car park and take a narrow path which passes through the line of posts marking its boundary to climb a slight slope straight ahead.

Follow the path to the road and cross it to take the metalled track giving access to Wilverley Plain car park and picnic place. At the T-junction turn right to walk through the car park and on along the track straight ahead keeping the inclosure on your left. This track is the old smugglers' road and will eventually lead you past the Naked Man which is enclosed by a wooden fence to protect it from the forest animals.

Having passed the Naked Man on the right, turn left through a gate into the inclosure. Follow the path straight ahead for about 25 yards to where it divides and then take the right-hand fork. This winds away through the trees and slowly widens into a track.

When you come to the place where this track is crossed by another turn right and walk up to the gate that gives access to the road. Do not go through the gate: turn sharp left beside it on to a track leading away from the road through the pine trees.

Carry straight on along this track to where it divides and then take the left-hand fork. This leads through the trees for a short distance before going down a steep slope at the bottom of which it is crossed by a second track. Ignore this and go up the slope straight ahead.

After some distance the track is joined by another from the left and at this point there is an interesting old inclosure sign on the right. This was placed here during the last century and gives a short account of the history of Wilverley Inclosure. Disregard the track to the left and carry straight on. This will lead you past a track which goes down a slope to the right and through a gate that opens on to the car park.

Walk 26   Bolderwood

4 miles (6 km)

OS sheet 195
Start: Highland Water Inclosure

The area around Bolderwood contains some of the most interesting
features to be found in the New Forest. Much of it has been laid out
by the Forestry Commission as a series of short forest walks and
sections of these have been incorporated into this ramble.

Beside the car park at Highland Water Inclosure is a simple wooden
cross. This was erected in April 1946 to commemorate the presence of
the 3rd Canadian Division of RCASC who were in this part of the
forest during World War II.

Not far from here is a deer sanctuary where the timid fallow deer,
which frequent large areas of the forest, can be seen. Although visitors
are not allowed to enter the sanctuary, wooden hides have been
erected for their convenience around the perimeter and these make
good vantage points from which to study the deer.

On one side the deer sanctuary is bordered by an arboretum containing an interesting selection of trees; it once formed part of the
grounds of the Master Keeper's lodge. This formerly stood near the
present keeper's cottage but was demolished in 1833.

In the woods near the arboretum stands the Radnor Stone. This is
a memorial stone to the Earl of Radnor and is beautifully decorated
with pictures of the forest animals and plants.

Turn off the A35 on the western edge of Lyndhurst on to the road
signposted 'Emery Down $\frac{1}{4}$'. Follow this to the New Forest Inn on the
left and then turn left on to a road marked 'Bolderwood 4 – Linwood
7'. Drive along this road for $3\frac{1}{2}$ miles and, having passed a road
junction on the left, turn right into the car park at the edge of Highland
Water Inclosure. The memorial to the 3rd Canadian Division of
RCASC is beside this car park on the right.

Start the walk by crossing the road to take the gravel track on the
opposite side. Ignore a track to the left and go straight ahead through
the vehicle barrier. Disregard two grassy tracks to the right and a
path to the left and continue to where the main track goes down a
slight slope and is crossed by another gravel one. Turn left on to this
and follow it, ignoring a path on the left, to where it is joined by
another path from the right just before it meets the road. Bear right
on to this path which skirts the trees on the right and then heads
towards the road. Just before it reaches it the path forks. Take the

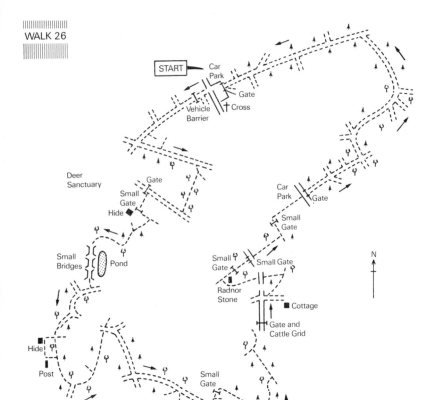

right-hand branch leading through the trees, keeping the road on your left.

This will bring you to where the path meets a gravel track. Turn right and follow the track down to the gate that gives access to the deer sanctuary. Do not go through the gate but turn left to keep the fence on your right. From here it is often possible to get good views of the deer within the sanctuary.

The fence will lead you to a small gate straight ahead beyond which there is a hide. Go through the gate and turn left to follow the fence on the left for about 20 yards before turning right on to a path that leads through the trees.

Within a very short distance the path merges with another from the right and then goes straight ahead for a little way before bearing right down a slope. At the bottom of the slope it swings left to pass over three small bridges and skirt a pond on the left. Just beyond the pond the path joins a track. Turn right on to this and where it forks keep to the left-hand branch. It swings round to the left and then divides again.

This time take the right-hand branch which soon degenerates into a path. Where it is crossed by another turn right. This will lead you to a second hide. Turn left beside it and walk along beside the fence on the right for about 50 yards to reach a place where there is a post bearing a Forestry Commission deer sanctuary sign. Turn left beside it and follow the fairly wide path leading away from the sanctuary.

After about 10 yards the path joins another in a T-junction. Turn right and follow this path through the trees. It swings left at a point where a track leads straight ahead. Ignore the track and continue along the path disregarding all side turnings until it crosses another track. Leave the path at this point and turn right to follow the track. Within a few yards the track divides. Take the right-hand fork. This goes through the trees to meet another gravel track at a point where a grassy track leads straight ahead. Turn left on to the gravel track.

Ignore two grassy paths to the right where the track turns left and continue along it until you come to a place where it is joined by a track from the right and a path leads towards a small gate on the left. Turn left on to this path and go through the gate then turn right to follow a grassy path keeping the fence on your right. Carry straight on until you come to another gate in the fence. This is larger than the previous gate. Turn left beside it to follow a path curving left up the slope, ignoring two others that lead to the right.

The path climbs diagonally up the slope to join another path at the top. Turn left on to this and continue along it until you come to the road ignoring another path which leads back down the slope to the left. Leave the path as it swings left again near the road and turn left to follow the verge. Go through the gate beside the cattle grid and carry straight on until you pass a white cottage beyond a field on the right. This is the keeper's cottage.

Cross the road at this point to take a track leading towards the cottage and then turn almost immediately left on to a path signposted 'Start of Forest Walk'. Follow this through the trees to where it is joined by another path from the left and then turn left. This path leads back to the road. Cross over and take the path straight ahead. It goes down a slope and then swings right to pass the Radnor Stone on the right.

Just beyond the stone the path meets another in a T-junction. Turn right on to this and follow it through a small gate and on to where it meets the road. Cross the road and take the path leading straight ahead to meet another path. Turn left on to this and go through the gate into a car park. Turn right to skirt the car park and cross another road and then go through the gate opening into the inclosure.

Follow the track straight ahead ignoring a grassy one crossing it at right-angles. The track goes down a slope. Disregard a grassy track to the left part of the way down and continue to where the track is crossed by another gravel one near the bottom. Turn left on to this and follow it, disregarding two tracks to the left and three to the right, until it eventually meets yet another gravel track in a T-junction. Turn left on to this and continue along it, ignoring all side turnings, until you come to a gate which leads out of the inclosure to the car park where you left the car.

Walk 27   Eyeworth Pond

6½ miles (10 km)

OS sheets 184 and 195
Start: Telegraph Hill car park

This walk is one of the best for those who wish to sample a variety of New Forest scenery. Parts of it run across open heathland whilst others lead through an inclosure of oak trees where many species of woodland birds are to be seen.

Eyeworth Pond is one of the New Forest beauty spots; a delightful stretch of water reserved as a water fowl conservancy. It is a very picturesque spot particularly in early summer when the water is starred with clumps of water lilies. Yet this has not always been the case. Eyeworth was once the site of a gunpowder factory. This was in operation during the latter half of the last century but today little evidence remains of it except a curious old post box situated at the Fritham end of the lane to Eyeworth.

Leave the M27 at junction 1 and take the B3078, signposted 'Fording-bridge'. Having turned left opposite The Bell in Brook village, continue to follow the road for just over 3 miles to where the B3078 and the B3080 diverge. Just before the junction turn left into Telegraph Hill car park.

Return to the road and turn left on to a track that leads through a vehicle barrier. Ignore a path which crosses it at right-angles and where the track divides take the left-hand fork. This goes through the edge of the wood and as it enters the trees it branches again. Still keep to the left fork and do the same again where the track branches for a third time.

Just beyond this the track is joined by two more from the right but still carry straight on. Ignore three grassy tracks to the left and where the main track forks take the right-hand branch. This will eventually bring you to a group of holly trees. A track leads away to the left but ignore it and carry straight on.

Disregard another track to the left, one to the right and a third that crosses the track you are following. Beyond this you will pass a small brick building on the right. Ignore a gravel track to the left just opposite it and a second to the right further on and continue to where the track meets another in a T-junction.

Turn left and follow the track down the slope. At the bottom it is joined by another track coming through a gate to the right. Ignore this and carry straight on disregarding two tracks to the left as the

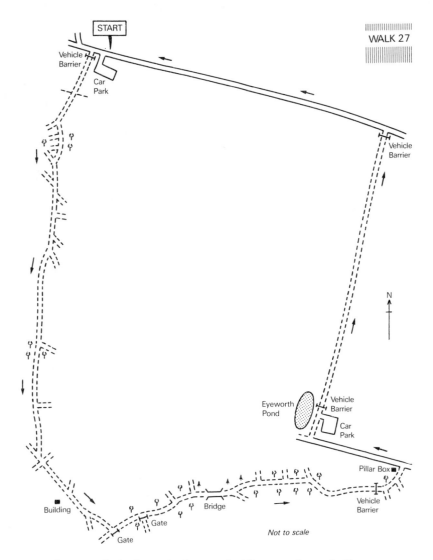

START

Vehicle Barrier

Car Park

Vehicle Barrier

N

Eyeworth Pond

Vehicle Barrier

Car Park

Pillar Box

Vehicle Barrier

Building

Bridge

Gate

Gate

Not to scale

main one winds through the wood. After crossing a bridge over a small stream the track swings sharp left at a point where a grassy track leads straight ahead. Ignore this grassy track and another three that join the gravel one to the left further on.

Just beyond the third of these the track emerges from the trees. It climbs a slope and passes through a vehicle barrier beyond which it is joined by another track from the right. Ignore this and carry straight on to follow the track round to the left where it meets a lane. Just beside the junction to the left is the old post box.

Turn left on to the lane and follow it down to Eyeworth Pond. Where the tarmac ends turn right on to a track which leads up to Eyeworth Pond car park, passing the pond on your left. Pass the car park on your right and take the track leading straight ahead through a vehicle barrier. This will eventually bring you to a road. Turn left and follow the verge back to Telegraph Hill where the car park is on the left.

Walk 28   Woodgreen

$3\frac{1}{2}$ miles (5.5 km)

OS sheet 184
Start: Godshill car park

The village of Woodgreen lies on the north-western edge of the New Forest at a point where the river Avon forms the forest boundary. It is bordered to the east by pleasant inclosures of mature soft and hardwood trees beyond which there are fine views across the open heathland towards Godshill.

To the south of the village is Castle Hill, thought to be the site of the only Norman fortification in the forest area. The hill slopes steeply down to the river at its foot and from the crest there is a magnificent view across the river valley towards Fordingbridge and Breamore.

Take the A338 from Ringwood travelling towards Salisbury and turn right in Breamore on to the road signposted 'Woodgreen 1 – Hale 3'. Having crossed the cattle grid at the beginning of Woodgreen village, take the first turning on the right passing the post office on your right and Rose Cottage on the left. This is the road to Godshill. Follow it for about a mile to where, having left the village behind, it swings sharp left and is joined by a gravel lane on the right. Just beyond this point turn right into Godshill car park.

Walk back to the car park entrance and turn left to follow the edge of the road. Leave it where it swings right and go along the gravel lane keeping the inclosure fence on your right. Within a short distance the gravel lane meets a metalled one coming up a slope from the left. Just past this point there is a gate in the inclosure fence on the right.

Go through the gate beyond which three paths diverge. Take the central one. It runs straight ahead through the trees and is crossed by a track. Ignore this and continue along the path. Disregard two paths on the left and one on the right and carry on to where the main path divides, then take the left-hand fork. This leads straight ahead and ends at a gate that opens on to the road at Castle Hill. Directly opposite and to the left are view points affording beautiful views of the Avon valley.

Having left the inclosure by the small gate turn right to follow the verge. Within about 100 yards the inclosure fence on the right comes to an end. Turn right at this point to take a narrow path which leads down a bank, keeping the inclosure fence on your right. This will soon bring you to another road. Cross it and go through a small gate

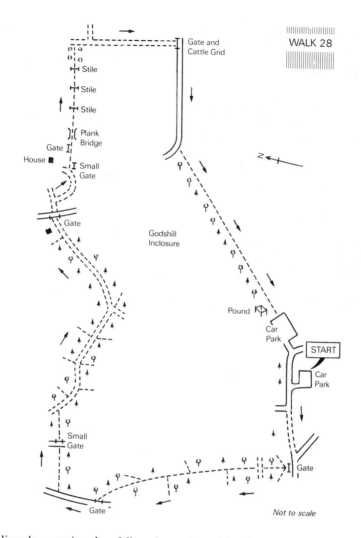

Gate and
Cattle Grid

Stile

Stile

Stile

Plank
Bridge

Gate

House

Small
Gate

Gate

Godshill
Inclosure

Pound

Car
Park

START

Car
Park

Small
Gate

Gate

Gate

Not to scale

directly opposite, then follow the path straight ahead. It leads through the trees to join a track.

Turn right and walk along the track, disregarding one path to the left, another to the right and two that cross it, until eventually you come to where the track merges with another in a T-junction. Turn left on to the track that forms the head of the 'T' and follow this to the gate at the edge of the inclosure.

Go through the gate and cross the road to take a track directly opposite, labelled 'Footpath'. The track curves to the right over a

99

cattle grid and then divides. Keep to the right-hand fork and where the track swings left to end at a house take the path straight ahead passing a small wooden gate on your right. The path leads past a large wooden gate on the left, over a small plank bridge and up a slope to a stile.

Cross this and the field beyond to reach a second stile in the fence on the far side. This gives access to another field. Walk straight across it to another stile in the hedge from which a narrow path leads down through the bushes to a track. Turn right to follow the track, ignoring another which is marked 'Footpath' and leads away to the left.

The track eventually meets the road in a T-junction. Turn right and walk along the edge of the road to where it swings sharp right towards Woodgreen. Leave the road at this point to take the path straight ahead with the inclosure fence on your right. This will eventually bring you to where a pound stands beside the inclosure fence. The pound is used when the animals that graze in the forest are rounded up for branding. It is rather dilapidated but well worth pausing to look at because some of the brand marks used by animals' owners are cut into the wood of one of the posts.

Having passed the pound on your right you will come to a car park. There are good views from here across the open heathland to the left. Walk straight ahead across the car park to the road and then bear right to follow the verge. This will bring you back to Godshill car park, on the left.

Walk 29   Breamore and the Mizmaze

4 miles (6 km)

OS sheet 184
Start: Breamore village

This is a pleasant walk through rolling downland countryside where many features of historical interest are to be seen but unfortunately it is not one on which you can take your dog. Parts of the route run through the Breamore Estate where dogs are not allowed.

Breamore is a small and picturesque village to the west of the river Avon. It lies in a valley bordered to the west by softly rounded hills that are really an extension of Salisbury Plain.

The church is the oldest in this part of Hampshire. It is the finest example of a Saxon church in the county and contains several interesting features. Above the south door is a badly damaged Saxon rood surmounted by the hand of God emerging from a cloud. The rood was deliberately mutilated at the time of the Reformation when the carving was cut back level with the wall. Another Saxon relic which escaped this kind of attention is a sentence carved into one of the four arches supporting the tower. It is one of the few Saxon inscriptions to be found in England and means 'Here the Covenant becomes manifest to thee'.

The mizmaze, situated in a grove of yew trees high on a hill above Breamore, is one of the most fascinating historical remains in Hampshire. There are only seven such mazes in the whole of England and the one at Breamore is in the best condition. It is over 30 yards in diameter and consists of a narrow grassy causeway which weaves its way between grooves of chalk to a central mound. Nobody knows its true age or original purpose but it is generally believed that it was used for some kind of religious rite by our pagan ancestors.

Breamore House, an imposing Tudor building, was skilfully restored after a fire in 1853. It was the home of the Hulse family for over two hundred years and today it contains a fine collection of paintings and furniture. During the summer months the house is often open to the public and there are an Agricultural Museum and a Carriage Museum in the grounds.

Turn off the A338 in Breamore village on to the lane signposted 'Whitsbury $3\frac{1}{2}$'. Drive along this for about 50 yards to park on the grass on the left just beyond the thatched cottages.

Walk on along the lane ignoring a gravel track to the left and where the lane forks take the left-hand branch. This continues to skirt the green on the left for a short distance before swinging right and eventually meeting another lane in a T-junction.

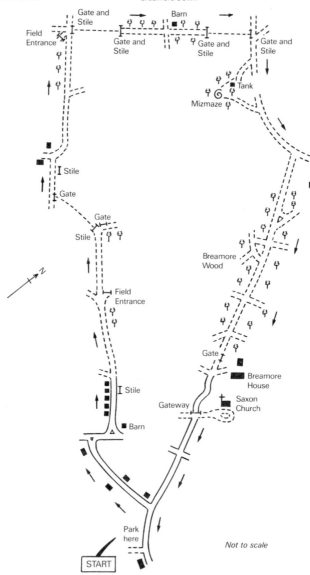

WALK 29

Breamore Down

Gate and Stile

Field Entrance

Barn

Gate and Stile

Gate and Stile

Gate and Stile

Tank

Mizmaze

Stile

Gate

Gate

Stile

Field Entrance

Breamore Wood

Gate

Stile

Breamore House

Gateway

Saxon Church

Barn

Park here

START

Not to scale

Turn right and then left on to a lane which passes a barn on the right. Follow the lane to where it ends and then take the track straight ahead ignoring a field entrance on the left. The track leads up a slight slope, bears left and then forks at a point where there is a field entrance on the right. Take the right-hand fork leading straight ahead.

Where the track turns sharp right beside the tip of a wood on the right turn left to cross a stile beside a field gate. This gives access to a narrow path running down between the fields to join a track in the valley. Turn right and follow the track which will take you past a farm on the left.

Some distance beyond this it forks. Keep to the left-hand branch leading straight ahead. After about $\frac{1}{2}$ mile the trees on the left give way to a short expanse of grass, the track becomes grass covered and is joined by another coming down a slope from the left. Turn right at this point to cross a stile beside a field gate and then follow the fence on the right up the slope towards the wood.

This will bring you to another field gate with a stile beside it giving access to a track. Follow the track straight ahead and where it is crossed by another keep the Dutch barn on your left and carry straight on through the wood. At the far side the track ends at a field gate. Go through this and on up the slope keeping the fence on your right. At the top there is another gate and stile with a track beyond.

Cross the stile and turn right to follow the track to where the fence on the right ends and the track forks. Take the right-hand branch leading up the slope towards the trees. Near the beginning of the wood a narrow, rather indistinct, path goes through a gap in the trees. Turn right on to this and enter the wood passing a rectangular metal tank on your left. Head straight through the trees to the clearing where you will find the mizmaze.

Turn left to skirt the mizmaze and leave it by a path to the left about a quarter of the way round. The path comes out of the wood and curves slightly right to join a track coming from the left. Turn right on to this and follow it as it curves to the left down the slope.

At the bottom it is joined by another track from the left. Ignore this and carry straight on. The track is now bordered by hedges and after a while it forks. Keep to the right-hand branch which is the major of the two. After a short distance it goes into a wood. Carry straight on ignoring all side turnings until the track eventually emerges from the trees. At this point it divides three ways. Take the central fork. This will lead you past Breamore House on the left. Ignore two tracks to the right near the house and carry on down the metalled drive to the gateway. Just beyond this a gravel track to the left leads to the Saxon church.

To continue the walk take the metalled lane straight ahead. Where this is crossed by another still go straight on following the lane sign-posted 'Breamore $\frac{3}{4}$'. This will bring you to where two lanes join. The parking place is straight ahead at the far end of the village green on the right.

3 miles (4.5 km)

OS sheet 184
Start: Martin Down

The open expanse of grassland known as Martin Down has not been part of Hampshire for very long. It came into the county during the late nineteenth century when the border between Hampshire and Wiltshire was altered slightly. In character it is much more like part of Wiltshire than Hampshire, being very similar to the neighbouring Salisbury Plain.

Today Martin Down is a National Nature Reserve and here are to be seen a variety of downland animals including the timid roe deer, the smallest species of deer to be found in the British Isles. They stand just over 2 feet tall at the shoulder and their antlers are at the maximum only 8 or 9 inches in length.

Martin Down also has several interesting historical features. One of these is Bokerley Ditch which runs along the western edge of the down marking the border between Hampshire and Dorset. This ditch and its attendant bank were built during Roman times to protect the area to the west of Martin Down from invasion.

To the east of it lies Grim's Ditch, another ancient earthwork consisting of two banks with a ditch between them. Much older then Bokerley Ditch it is thought to date from the Middle Bronze Age.

Turn off the A354 on to the road signposted 'Martin 1½ – Damerham 4½ – Fordingbridge 8'. Drive into Martin village and take the second turning on the left, just beyond a small shop called The Central Stores. Follow this lane to where the tarmac ends and park on the grass straight ahead. Leave the car park by the track to the right, signposted 'Blagdon Gap'. This skirts the hedge on the right.

Ignore two tracks to the left and where the main track divides keep to the left-hand fork. This is slightly wider than the right-hand one and runs parallel to it for some distance before dividing again. Take either branch for they both descend the slope and then rejoin at a point where six tracks meet. Turn on to the first track on the left. It climbs a sharp slope skirting an earthwork on the left. This is Grim's Ditch.

Ignore an overgrown track to the right and carry straight on to where the track is crossed by another. Turn left on to this. It cuts across Grim's Ditch and then leads down a slope into a valley. Here it is crossed by another track but ignore this and continue up the next

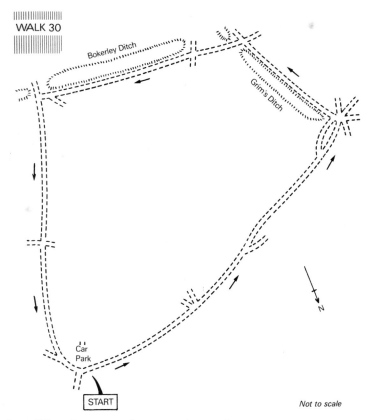

Bokerley Ditch

Grim's Ditch

N

Car Park

START

Not to scale

slope. There is now another, more impressive, earthwork on the right. This is Bokerley Ditch and at this point it forms the border between Hampshire and Dorset.

Near the top of the slope the track is joined by another from the left but ignore this and carry straight on for a short distance to where the track merges with another which cuts through the earthwork to the right. This is on the crest of the down and there is a magnificent view across the valley to the left where Martin village nestles between Martin Down and Toyd Down. It is also a very good vantage point from which to spot the deer and other wild creatures that frequent the downs.

Continue the walk by turning left on to the track which has cut through Bokerley Ditch. Follow it down the slope to the valley and ignore another track crossing it at right-angles near the bottom of the hill. From here the track continues straight ahead to join a gravel one. Turn left on to it and within a very short distance you will be back at the place where you left the car.